Epic Journey
The Life and Times of Wasyl Kushnir

Epic Journey
The Life and Times of Wasyl Kushnir

ANDREI KUSHNIR

BOSTON
2020

Library of Congress Cataloging-in-Publication Data

Names: Kushnir, Andrei, author.
Title: Epic journey : the life and times of Wasyl Kushnir / Andrei Kushnir.
Other titles: Life and times of Wasyl Kushnir
Description: Boston : Academic Studies Press, 2020.
Identifiers: LCCN 2019054275 (print) | LCCN 2019054276 (ebook) | ISBN 9781644691090 (hardback) | ISBN 9781644691106 (paperback) | ISBN 9781644691113 (adobe pdf)
Subjects: LCSH : Kushnir, Wasyl Andreievych, 1923-2019. | Kushnir, Wasyl Andreievych, 1923-2019--Correspondence. | Ukrainian Americans--Biography. | Ukraine--Biography. | Ukraine--Politics and government--1917-1945. | World War, 1939-1945--Conscript labor--Germany.
Classification: LCC E184.U5 K825 2020 (print) | LCC E184.U5 (ebook) | DDC 947.708092 [B]--dc23
LC record available at https://lccn.loc.gov/2019054275
LC ebook record available at https://lccn.loc.gov/2019054276

Copyright © 2020 Academic Studies Press
All rights reserved.

ISBN 978-1-644691-09-0 (hardback)
ISBN 978-1-644691-10-6 (paperback)
ISBN 978-1-644691-11-3 (adobe pdf)
ISBN 978-1-644693-71-1 (ePub)

Book design by Lapiz Digital Services.
Cover design by Ivan Grave.

Published by Cherry Orchard Books (imprint of Academic Studies Press)
1577 Beacon Street
Brookline, MA 02446, USA
press@academicstudiespress.com
www.academicstudiespress.com

Contents

Acknowledgments	ix
List of Illustrations	x
Introduction	xix
Family History	1
Dispossession and Father's Arrest	6
My Mother's Travails	11
My Life After the Arrests of My Parents	14
The Holodomor	16
My Parents, and Their Lives During and After the Holodomor	20
I Rejoin My Parents	24
Uncle Danylo	25
Life with My Parents in Bilychi	30
The German Army Enters Kyiv	33
Return to Nova Bubnivka	35
Conscription to Forced Labor in Germany	37
Correspondence I Received as a Forced Laborer in Germany	41
Postcard 1. June 27, 1943	42
Postcard 2. June 27, 1943	43
Postcard 3. July 2, 1943	44
Postcard 4. July 11, 1943	45
Postcard 5. July 28, 1943	46
Postcard 6. July 28, 1943	47

Postcard 7. August 1, 1943	48
Postcard 8. August 7, 1943	49
Postcard 9. August 13, 1943	50
Postcard 10. August 13, 1943	51
Postcard 11. August 22, 1943	52
Postcard 12. September 3, 1943	53
Postcard 13. September 4, 1943	54
Postcard 14. September 11, 1943	55
Postcard 15. September 12, 1943	57
Postcard 16. September 11, 1943	58
Postcard 17. September 12, 1943	59
Postcard 18. October 3, 1943	60
Postcard 19. October 31, 1943	61
Postcard 20. October 31, 1943	62
Postcard 21. November 28, 1943	63
Postcard 22. November 28, 1943	64
Postcard 23. February 16, 1944	65
Postcard 24. May 7, 1944	66
The War Ends; I Am Set Free	67
Life in the Refugee Camp, Regensburg, Germany	69
I Start My Own Family	78
We Immigrate to the United States	84
Life in Chicago	88
Reconnecting with my Mother	99
Family Life in Chicago	100
Move to Palatine, Illinois	108
Our Family in America	110
Our Move to Florida. The Family Grows	113
Last Thoughts	120
Postscript	121

For my mother, Maria, brothers Anatolij and Wolodymyr, and sister Nadia, with whom I shared the easiest and happiest part of my father Wasyl's journey.

Acknowledgments

I express my sincere thanks to Ekaterina Yanduganova for her kind assistance in placing this manuscript in the hands of Academic Studies Press; Stuart Allen for his editing assistance; my brothers Anatolij and Wolodymyr Kushnir and sister Nadia Kushnir Chomko for their reading and comments on the manuscript; Dr. Oleh Kotsyuba for introducing me to the Academic Studies Press team and other recommendations, Dr. Serhii Plokhii for his initial evaluation of this project; Raya Shadursky for her understanding and support of this project; Peter Yarrow, renowned folksinger and founder of Operation Respect and other humanitarian activities, for his endorsement and help; and the Ukrainian Jewish Encounter Board of Directors for their assistance with subvention costs. Most of all, I want to thank my father, Wasyl Kushnir, for his determination to tell his story in its fullness, to share his and his family's darkest as well as proudest moments, and also my mother, Maria Kushnir, who bore the burden of living with my father's driven desire to preserve the history of their experiences, covering almost a century. I accept gladly the blame for any shortcomings herein.

A note regarding spelling: the English spelling of Ukrainian words and names has created difficulties for translators, writers, reporters, map makers, scholars, and historians for the past two centuries. Transliteration is challenging because many Ukrainian sounds do not have direct counterparts in English, not to mention that English often ascribes similar sounds to different alphabet letters, and different sounds to similar letters. Thus, I have used the English spellings of Ukrainian names that correspond with official documents when such documents exist, and the spellings of Ukrainian, Russian, or Polish names, places, and words as I have seen to appear in those English publications I have consulted in drafting the manuscript. In cases where no documentary sources were available, the Ukrainian soft sign is not rendered in transliterations of proper names for ease of reading, but retained in common nouns, and letter й is usually rendered as i. Letters such as ю and я are rendered as yu and ya, except for women's names, which end in -ia rather than -iya.

The editors at Academic Studies Press have been of invaluable help in ensuring correctness and consistency. If some errors or inconsistencies nevertheless appear, I humbly assume responsibility for them.

List of Illustrations

1. My father, Andrei Semenovych Kushnir, 1896–1944. Unknown date and photographer.
2. Symon Petliura, Head of the Directorate of Ukrainian National Republic, Chief of Military Forces of Ukrainian National Army. Unknown date and photographer. Image in the United States Public Domain. Wikimedia Commons.
3. Map of Ukraine, showing the approximate location of the village of Nova Bubnivka. Sven Teschke, Paweł Marynowski, Creative Commons Attribution-Share Alike 3.0 license. Used with the authors' permission.
4. Gravestone of my Grandfather, Semen Vasylevych Kushnir, 1871–1919. Photograph by Wasyl Kushnir, September 1994.
5. Wasyl Kushnir, at the gravesite of Semen Vasylevych Kushnir, village of Nova Bubnivka, Ukraine, September 1994. Note the broken sections of the gravestone, destroyed by Communist activists in 1930. Photograph by Maria Kushnir.
6. Maria Kushnir, wife of Wasyl Kushnir, and Raissa Yaremchuk, cousin to Wasyl Kushnir, at the gravesite of Semen Vasylevych Kushnir, September 1994. Photograph by Wasyl Kushnir.
7. My mother, Anna Yakivna Pidkaliuk Kushnir, 1902–1988. Unknown date and photographer.
8. The Kushnir family, June 20, 1930. Andrei, Wasyl, Halyna Pidkalyuk (Anna's niece, and Wasyl's cousin), Anna. Unknown photographer.
9. *The National Tribune*, a Ukrainian-language newspaper published in the United States, on December 6, 2009, on page 3, published a partial listing of persons of Ukrainian nationality who had been sentenced to the Steplag concentration camps by the Communist authorities during the years 1920–1950. My father's name appears near the middle of the listing on the right side of the page. Permission granted by the publisher.
10. This list in *The National Tribune*, which includes persons whose last names began with letters from KU to LA, contains the name of my father, Andrei Semenovych Kushnir, born in 1889 in the Vinnytsya oblast. The date cited is erroneous: my father was born in 1896. Permission granted by the publisher.
11. Ivan Yakivych Pidkalyuk, Anna Kushnir's brother. Unknown date and photographer.
12. Father's certificate of employment.
13. My mother, Anna Yakivna Kushnir, 1931. Unknown photographer.
14. My uncle, Danylo Semenovych Kushnir. Unknown date and photographer.
15. My grandmother, Yaryna Kushnir, 1966. Unknown photographer.
16. Saverko, last name unknown, as a soldier in the Soviet army, 1947. Unknown photographer.

17. *Daily Express* [London] headline, August 7, 1934. Public Domain, Wikimedia Commons.
18. Officials on a villager's property, looking for hidden food. Photograph provided by Holodomor Research and Education Consortium, CIUS, Alberta.
19. Victims of the Holodomor in Kharkiv. Photograph provided by Holodomor Research and Education Consortium, CIUS, Alberta.
20. Halyna and Wasyl Besarab, 1965. Unknown photographer.
21. First class of Bilychi sub-middle school, 1931–38. Wasyl Kushnir's photo is in the bottom middle. Unknown photographer.
22. A close-up of Wasyl Kushnir in the school photo. Unknown photographer.
23. Postcard from my uncle, Danylo Kushnir, dated June 1, 1941, front.
24. Postcard from my uncle, Danylo Kushnir, dated June 1, 1941, back side.
25. Letter dated May 15, 2012 to Andrei Kushnir, USA, from the State Archives, Khmelnytskyi Region, Khmelnytskyi Regional State Administration.
26. "Wasyl Kushnir, churchgoer, goes to pray at the Baikov cemetery in Kyiv." Facsimile drawing by Wasyl Kushnir.
27. Wasyl Kushnir. Unknown date and photographer.
28. Wasyl Kushnir and father, Andrei Kushnir, May 5, 1937. Unknown photographer.
29. Wasyl Kushnir, 1938. Unknown photographer.
30. Drawing of an OST patch by Wasyl Kushnir.
31. The Marschaleks. Unknown date and photographer.
32. A memorial card for their son, Franz, killed in the Second World War, front and back side.
33. Wasyl Kushnir, July 24, 1944. Unknown photographer.
34. Postcard 1, dated June 27, 1943, front.
35. Postcard 1, dated June 27, 1943, back.
36. Postcard 2, dated June 27, 1943, front.
37. Postcard 2, dated June 27, 1943, back.
38. Postcard 3, dated July 2, 1943, front.
39. Postcard 3, dated July 2, 1943, back.
40. Postcard 4, dated July 11, 1943, front.
41. Postcard 4, dated July 11, 1943, back.
42. Postcard 5, dated July 28, 1943, front.
43. Postcard 5, dated July 28, 1943, back
44. Postcard 6, dated July 28, 1943, front.
45. Postcard 6, dated July 28, 1943, back.
46. Postcard 7, dated August 1, 1943, front.
47. Postcard 7, dated August 1, 1943, back.
48. Postcard 8, dated August 7, 1943, front.
49. Postcard 8, dated August 7, 1943, back.
50. Postcard 9, dated August 13, 1943, front.

51. Postcard 9, dated August 13, 1943, back.
52. Postcard 10, dated August 13, 1943, front.
53. Postcard 10, dated August 13, 1943, back.
54. Postcard 11, dated August 22, 1943, front.
55. Postcard 11, dated August 22, 1943, back.
56. Postcard 12, dated September 3, 1943, front.
57. Postcard 12, dated September 3, 1943, back.
58. Wasyl's uncle Ivan (his mother Anna's brother), cousin Raissa, and Raissa's husband Andrei Yaremchuk, February 12, 1945. Unknown photographer.
59. Raissa Yaremchuk, her second husband (name unknown), and daughters Marina, Lena, and Lyudmila, 1991. Unknown photographer. Raissa died around 2010.
60. Postcard 13, dated September 4, 1943, front.
61. Postcard 13, dated September 4, 1943, back.
62. Postcard 14, dated September 11, 1943, front.
63. Postcard 14, dated September 11, 1943, back.
64. Postcard 15, dated September 12, 1943, front.
65. Postcard 15, dated September 12, 1943, back.
66. Postcard 16, dated September 11, 1943, front.
67. Postcard 16, dated September 11, 1943, back.
68. Postcard 17, dated September 12, 1943, front.
69. Postcard 17, dated September 12, 1943, back.
70. Postcard 18, dated October 3, 1943, front.
71. Postcard 18, dated October 3, 1943, back.
72. Postcard 19, dated October 31, 1943, front.
73. Postcard 19, dated October 31, 1943, back.
74. Postcard 20, dated October 31, 1943, front.
75. Postcard 20, dated October 31, 1943, back.
76. Postcard 21, dated November 28, 1943, front.
77. Postcard 21, dated November 28, 1943, back.
78. Postcard 22, dated November 28, 1943, front.
79. Postcard 22, dated November 28, 1943, back.
80. Postcard 23, dated February 16, 1944, front.
81. Postcard 23, dated February 16, 1944, back.
82. Postcard 24, dated May 7, 1944, front.
83. Postcard 24, dated May 7, 1944, back.
84. Ivan Pidkalyuk with children Olha and Victor. Unknown date and photographer.
85. Ivan Pidkalyuk's funeral, Chernyava, 1963. Unknown photographer.
86. Regensburg, Germany, circa 1947. Photograph by Wasyl Kushnir.
87. Ganghofer-Siedlung, circa 1947. Photograph by Wasyl Kushnir.

List of Illustrations | xiii

88. Ukrainian Center, Regensburg, circa 1947. Photograph by Wasyl Kushnir.
89. Ukrainian Center, Regensburg, circa 1947. Photograph by Wasyl Kushnir.
90. Streets in Ganghofer-Siedlung, circa 1947. Photograph by Wasyl Kushnir
91. Streets in Ganghofer-Siedlung, circa 1947, Photograph by Wasyl Kushnir
92. Identification document issued by Ukrainian Committee, August 24, 1945.
93. Registration with German police, June 11, 1945.
94. Registration with German police, July 25, 1945.
95. German police document confirming documentation was stolen, July 13, 1945.
96. Temporary registration card, August 4, 1945.
97. Permission to enter and leave the military quadrangle, signed Capt. George A. Gauthier, U.S. Army, August 14, 1945.
98. Permission letter, signed H. J. Schlouch, M. Sgt., U.S. Army, November 17, 1945.
99. Recommendation letter, Capt. G. A. Gauthier, U.S. Army, October 2, 1945
100. Mechanic identification card, December 1, 1945.
101. Left, U.S. Army identification card fragment, dated December 6, 1945. Right, German identification card, undated.
102. Recommendation, John D. Boyce, 1st Lt., Cav., U.S. Army, March 13, 1946.
103. Wasyl Kushnir and other drivers, Headquarters, 1049 Labor Supervision Company, 1945. Unknown photographer.
104. Wasyl Kushnir with three other drivers, 1049 Labor Supervision Company, circa 1947–1948. Unknown photographer.
105. Wasyl Kushnir, circa 1944. Unknown photographer.
106. Wasyl Kushnir with unknown man, circa 1945. Unknown photographer.
107. Wasyl Kushnir with an ambulance truck, 1945. Unknown photographer.
108. Wasyl Kushnir, 1945. Unknown photographer.
109. Wasyl Kushnir, 1945. Unknown photographer.
110. Wasyl Kushnir, January 16, 1946. Unknown photographer.
111. Wasyl Kushnir and 2¾-ton truck. Unknown date and photographer.
112. Wasyl Kushnir and 2¾-ton truck. Unknown date and photographer.
113. Wasyl Kushnir, Headquarters, 1049 Labor Supervision Company, Regensburg, 1948. Unknown photographer.
114. Wasyl Kushnir and Petro Kosmyna, circa 1946. Unknown photographer.
115. Anastasia Pawlishchiw Kosmyna, circa 1945. Unknown photographer.
116. Plast girls in formation, Regensburg, circa 1945. Photograph by Wasyl Kushnir.
117. Maria (top) with friends, circa 1945. Photograph by Wasyl Kushnir.
118. Maria Pawlishchiw, April 1942. Unknown photographer.
119. Maria in Plast uniform, July 22, 1946. Unknown photographer.
120. Maria, circa 1945. Photograph by Wasyl Kushnir.
121. Maria and Wasyl Kushnir, August 1, 1946, Regensburg, Unknown photographer.
122. Nurse and Maria Kushnir holding son Andrei, 1947. Photograph by Wasyl Kushnir.

123. Maria and Andrei Kushnir, circa 1948. Photograph by Wasyl Kushnir.
124. Andrei Kushnir with rabbits, Regensburg, circa 1948. Photograph by Wasyl Kushnir.
125. Andrei Kushnir, circa 1948. Photo by Wasyl Kushnir.
126. Maria, Andrei, and Wasyl Kushnir, circa 1948. Unknown photographer.
127. Commendation letter, by Wm. R. Gentry, 1st Lt. Cav. Motor Officer, U.S. Army, September 9, 1949.
128. Boarding the train to Amberg, Germany. First row left to right: unknown woman, unknown man, Petro Kosmyna (with hat), Anastasia Kosmyna, Maria Kushnir holding Andrei Kushnir, unknown woman, Petrick Kosmyna. Unknown boy and woman in front. Photograph by Wasyl Kushnir.
129. Train from Regensburg to Amberg, Germany, 1949. Photograph by Wasyl Kushnir.
130. Anatolij Kushnir. Photograph by Wasyl Kushnir.
131. Wasyl and Maria Kushnir, with Andrei (carried) and Anatolij (in baby carriage), Amberg, 1949. Photograph by Petro Jarochym, Andrei's godfather.
132. SAS airplane on which we flew to the United States, March 1, 1950. Photograph by Wasyl Kushnir.
133. Bus tickets to Mississippi, account, and receipt for purchases at Delta & Pine Land Co, 1950.
134. Delta & Pine Land Company, Scott, Mississippi, photographer Marion Post Wolcott. Public Domain.
135. Delta & Pine Land Company, Scott, Mississippi, 1939. Courtesy of The New York Public Library, Schomburg Center for Research in Black Culture, Photographs and Prints Division.
136. Photograph of the Karpa family by Wasyl Kushnir.
137. Letter of recommendation for Wasyl Kushnir issued by Delta & Pine Land Co., June 16, 1950.
138. The building at 1511 N. Milwaukee Avenue, 2012. Photograph by Andrei Kushnir.
139. Milwaukee Avenue, from 1511 building, looking north, 2012. Photograph by Andrei Kushnir.
140. Anatolij, Andrei, and Maria Kushnir, with Chrysler, on Potomac St., 1952. Photograph by Wasyl Kushnir.
141. Andrei, Maria, and Anatolij, 1952. Photograph by Wasyl Kushnir.
142. Maria with Andrei and Anatolij in Wicker Park, 1953. Photograph by Wasyl Kushnir.
143. Anastasia & Petro Kosmyna. Photograph by Wasyl Kushnir.
144. Maria, Anatolij, and Andrei Kushnir on stairs, 1735 Potomac Street. Photograph by Wasyl Kushnir.
145. Our block on Potomac Street, 1950s. Photograph by Wasyl Kushnir.
146. Maria, Anatolij, and Andrei Kushnir, with new Ford in Humboldt Park, 1953 or 1954. Photograph by Wasyl Kushnir.
147. 1731 W. Potomac Street, Chicago, Illinois. 2012. Photograph by Andrei Kushnir.
148. 2734 Haddon Avenue, Chicago, Illinois. 1957. Photograph by Wasyl Kushnir.
149. Living room at 2734 Haddon Ave., circa 1958. Photograph by Wasyl Kushnir.
150. Wasyl and daughter Nadia, 1957. Photograph by Maria Kushnir.
151. Nadia Kushnir, circa 1958. Photograph by Wasyl Kushnir.
152. Anatolij, Nadia, Maria, and Andrei, 1957. Photographer Wasyl Kushnir.
153. St. Volodymyr Ukrainian Orthodox Cathedral, Oakley and Cortex Streets. Unknown date and photographer.
154. St. Volodymyr Parish Ukrainian School, 1965. Unknown photographer.
155. Anatolij's First Communion, St. Volodymyr Parish, Pastor: Very Rev. Fedir Bilecky, 1956. Photograph by Wasyl Kushnir. Anatolij is in the white shirt, on left side.

156. Christening of our daughter Nadia at St. Volodymyr Ukrainian Orthodox Cathedral, Pastor: Very Rev. Fedir Bilecky. Photograph by Wasyl Kushnir.
157. Ukrainian language student concert, Church Hall, St. Volodymyr Ukrainian Orthodox Cathedral, circa 1956. Photograph by Wasyl Kushnir.
158. Ukrainian language play, Church Hall, St. Volodymyr Ukrainian Orthodox Cathedral, circa 1966. Photograph by Wasyl Kushnir.
159. Ukrainian language poetry reading, Church Hall, St. Volodymyr Ukrainian Orthodox Cathedral, circa 1966. Photograph by Wasyl Kushnir.
160. Andrei's Ukrainian class at St. Volodymyr Ukrainian Orthodox Cathedral, circa 1966. Unknown photographer. Andrei is in the white shirt in the middle of the back row. The teacher, Prof. Antin Kushchynskij, is on the right at the end of the row.
161. Captive Nations parade, circa 1958. Photograph by Wasyl Kushnir.
162. Captive Nations parade, circa 1958. Photograph by Wasyl Kushnir.
163. Captive Nations parade, circa 1958. Photograph by Wasyl Kushnir.
164. Captive Nations parade, circa 1958. Photograph by Wasyl Kushnir.
165. Katerina Ilyashenko (Andrei's godmother), holding Andrei, Wasyl Kushnir, Maria Kushnir (holding Anatolij), July 8, 1951 in Newark, NJ. Photograph by Mykola Ilyashenko.
166. Kushnir Family, Fishing in Wisconsin, 1957. Photograph by Mykola Ilyashenko.
167. Anatolij, Andrei, and Maria Kushnir on a Wisconsin farm owned by family friends, the Czajka family, 1956. Photograph by Wasyl Kushnir.
168. Anatolij and I also went ice skating on the Humboldt Park lagoon in the winter. Photograph by Andrei Kushnir.
169. When Andrei took up playing the guitar, we shopped in downtown Chicago until we bought just the guitar he wanted. Photograph by Anatolij Kushnir.
170. Photograph of my grandmother Yaryna and Anna Kushnir, circa 1956. Unknown photographer.
171. Anatolij, Wasyl, Wolodymyr, Nadia, circa 1964. Photograph by Andrei Kushnir.
172. Nadia, 1961. Photograph by Wasyl Kushnir.
173. Nadia's birthday party, 1965. Photograph by Wasyl Kushnir.
174. Nadia and Wolodymyr, 1961. Photograph by Wasyl Kushnir
175. Wasyl Kushnir, Real Estate Salesman License, April 3, 1959.
176. Wolodymyr, June 1961. Photograph by Wasyl Kushnir
177. Wolodymyr, 1970. Photograph by Wasyl Kushnir.
178. The building at 2525 N. St. Louis Ave. Photograph by Wasyl Kushnir.
179. The building at 3339 West Crystal Street. Photograph by Wasyl Kushnir.
180. Anastasia Kosmyna, Nadia Kushnir, Anna Kushnir, circa 1968. Photograph by Wasyl Kushnir.
181. The Kushnir Family, circa 1968. Front row: Wolodymyr, Anna, Nadia. Back row: Andrei, Maria, Wasyl and Anatolij. Photographer: Darc Studios, Chicago, no successor in interest.
182. The building on Chicago Avenue, circa 2014. Photographer unknown.
183. Wasyl Kushnir, Real Estate Broker License, May 9, 1968.

184. Twenty-fifth wedding anniversary party, 1971. Photograph by Bohdan Chomko.
185. Wasyl Kushnir in orchard at Palatine, Illinois property, circa 1990. Photograph by Wolodymyr Kushnir.
186. Anna Kushnir, circa 1980. Photograph by Wasyl Kushnir.
187. Andrei's in-laws, Stefan and Anna Shyshko, with Wasyl Kushnir, on the Palatine, Illinois property, circa 1980. Photograph by Andrei Kushnir.
188. Wasyl Kushnir, Notary Public Certificate, February 21, 1984.
189. Andrei was an attorney with the Office of General Counsel, United States Navy, and one of his assignments was Counsel, U.S. Naval Supply Depot, Yokosuka, Japan 1984–86. Andrei is on the far right, first row. Unknown photographer.
190. One of Andrei's projects in Japan was supporting the reconditioning of a United States Navy aircraft carrier, 1986. Unknown photographer.
191. Andrei Kushnir painting in Telluride, Colorado, 2017. Photograph by Tash Montlake. Permission granted.
192. Anatolij Kushnir, Attorney, U.S. Department of Interior, 1973. Unknown photographer.
193. Anatolij Kushnir, 2010. Unknown photographer.
194. At the Taras Shevchenko monument, Washington, D.C., circa 1990. Unknown photographer.
195. Larissa acting in Ukrainian school play, circa 1991. Unknown photographer.
196. Anatolij (third from left in back row) and Andrei (fourth from left in front row) with the Rector of the National University of Internal Affairs, Colonel-General of Police, and National Deputy of Ukraine, Oleksandr M. Bandurka, 1993. Other members of the North American consortium were Michael Simmons, attorney (second from left in back row), Edward J. Melanson, former U.S. Ambassador (third from left in front row), and Gregory Shyshko, Canadian oil company executive (first from left in front row). Unknown photographer.
197. Maria Kushnir, Englewood Beach, Forida, 2010. Photograph by Raissa Kushnir.
198. Wasyl Kushnir, Englewood Beach, Florida, 2010. Photograph by Raissa Kushnir.
199. Maria, Wasyl and Andrei Kushnir, Manasota Key, 2010. Photograph by Raissa Kushnir.
200. Maria and Wasyl Kushnir with daughter Nadia, Englewood Beach, 2013. Photograph by Raissa Kushnir.
201. Andrei and wife Raissa, 1971. Unknown photographer.
202. Anatolij and wife Jaroslava. Photograph by Andrei Kushnir.
203. Nadia and husband Bohdan. Unknown photographer.
204. Wolodymyr and wife Larysa. Photograph by Andrei Kushnir.
205. Members of the Kushnir family in Englewood, Florida, August 1993. Back row, L to R: Bohdan Chomko (Nadia's husband), Wasyl, Anatolij, Jaroslava (Anatolij's wife). Middle row, L to R: Nadia holding son Gregory, Maria, Raissa (Andrei's wife). Front row, L to R: Larissa (Andrei's daughter), Basil (Andrei's son), Andrei, Wolodymyr. Photograph by Andrei Kushnir.
206. Members of the Kushnir family on the veranda in Englewood, Florida, 2012. Back row, L to R: Andrei, Wasyl, Anatolij, and Wolodymyr. Front row, L to R: Nadia, Raissa (Andrei's wife), Maria, Larysa (Wolodymyr's wife). Photograph by Andrei Kushnir.
207. L to R: grandson Basil, great granddaughter Sophie, Wasyl, Maria, great granddaughter Lilia, grandson Basil's wife Melissa, 2011. Photograph by Basil Kushnir.

208. Front row, L to R: Maria, daughter Nadia, grandson Gregory, Nadia's husband, Bohdan. Back row, L to R: Wasyl, Nadia's son Alexander, sons Andrei, Anatolij, Wolodymyr, Wolodymyr's wife Larysa, 2010. Photograph by Andrei Kushnir.
209. The new generation: Gregory and Alexander, sons of our daugher Nadia and son-in-law Bohdan Chomko. Photograph by Anatolij Kushnir.
210. The new generation: Sophie, Anastasia, and Lilia, daughters of our grandson Basil and his wife Melissa. Photograph by Melissa Kushnir.
211. The new generation: Russell Andrei, son of our granddaughter Larissa and her husband Wesley Davis, 2015. Unknown photographer.
212. Taras Shevchenko's museum, Kaniv, 1994. Unknown photographer.
213. Olha Vronska and Maria Kushnir, 1994. Photograph by Wasyl Kushnir.
214. Wasyl Kushnir, Golden Gate of Kyiv, 1994. Photograph by Maria Kushnir.
215. Maria and Wasyl Kushnir, with two others, at Taras Shevchenko's gravesite monument, Kaniv, 1994. Unknown photographer.
216. Maria and Wasyl Kushnir, Englewood, Florida, 2014. Photograph by Raissa Kushnir.

Introduction

After some fifty years of listening to reminiscences by my father, Wasyl Kushnir, and realizing that I quickly forgot important details, even after a few days, I suggested that he write out his recollections about his life growing up in Ukraine. He produced a thirty-page longhand manuscript in dense Ukrainian language and subsequently added another fifteen pages or so. Remarkably, his narrative was succinct and interesting enough to read through, and I had no trouble translating it into English, except for a few words that relate to farm implements and such. This handwritten text, as translated, supplemented with information learned from further questions and edited by myself, Mr. Oles Tymoshenko, his mother, Ms. Yaryna Antonenko-Davydovych Tymoshenko,[1] and Mr. Oles Tymoshenko's nephew, also named Oles Tymoshenko (a Ukrainian Orthodox priest in the Kyiv area), is presented in my father's voice and comprises the first section of this book.

A second section quotes from a series of postcards containing correspondence from his father in 1943, and a few other such postcards that he miraculously preserved through his time as a conscripted forced laborer in Germany, and subsequently. The text of these documents is raw history of life in Ukraine and Germany during the German occupation of Ukraine. These postcards contain honest glimpses of my father's past life in the village, the lives of his parents who remained, their parental concern for my father's welfare in Germany, their preoccupation with the details of beekeeping and farming to produce the grain and food they would need to survive, life in their village under the occupation, the breakdown of society when the German troops began retreating (particularly the last several postcards), and the difficult life of his cousin Ivan, who was conscripted by the Germans to labor in a coal mine. This section should be read carefully and savored for its accuracy, as it is truly unedited historical text. I am indebted for the assistance provided me in the translations and formatting of the postcards by Rev. Oles Tymoshenko, mentioned above.

The third section is a summary narrative of my father's life in the United States of America, also in his voice, and which is taken from verbal reminiscences and documents, and which he personally considered accurate, after

---

[1] See the top of page 9 of the *Ukrainian Weekly*, July 22, 1990, http://www.ukrweekly.com/archive/1990/The_Ukrainian_Weekly_1990-29.pdf.

reading through my narrative in his ninetieth year. The Rev. Oles Tymoshenko performed the translations in this last section.

This account of my father's life, while harrowing and often inspirational, is probably not exceptional, but representative of the strife, and indeed horrors, experienced by millions of Ukrainians who lived through the years of Moscow's Communist domination and exploitation of Ukraine and its people. My father's struggle to establish a more "normal" existence in the United States and his success in raising a family and living a productive life in American society demonstrates the potential that was lost to Ukrainian society during the over seventy years of totalitarian Communist rule. This narrative is provided to help the people of Ukraine to better understand their recent history, for the future generations of our family, and to demonstrate to my father's adopted American homeland the spirit, courage, and perseverance of the people of Ukrainian ancestry who came to live here and contribute to the greatness of the American nation.

Andrei Kushnir

Family History

My grandfather,[1] Semen Vasylevich Kushnir, was a completely illiterate *batrak* [farm laborer], who worked for wealthier people. At the age of twenty, he married a girl, Yaryna, from a very poor family. He made a little money, and purchased a two hectare parcel of land in the *selo*, or village, of Nova [in English, New] Bubnivka. The *selo*'s original name was just Bubnivka, after the Ukrainian word for banging on a drum, taken from the drumming of Turks or Mongols who occupied those lands during a period in the distant past. Later, many Polish families moved into the area, encouraged by the Polish government, and claimed most lots in the village, and the name was changed to Nova Bubnivka. While the *selo*, comprising some twenty or thirty houses along two streets, was located in Ukraine, most of its inhabitants were of Polish nationality.

The Kushnir family had lived in the *selo* for many generations. My grandfather Semen built a house and began a household. He and Yaryna had twelve children, one every year, but over half of them did not survive childhood. The eldest son was my father, Andrei Semenovych. He had two brothers, Avksentij and Danylo, and two sisters, Domakha and Ksenia.

During the First World War, my grandfather Semen served in the Russian tsarist army. My father Andrei was called to serve as well, and had the rank of sub-officer in the tsarist army. My father had completed his middle education in a gymnasium. My grandfather and father were stationed on the Austrian-German front, at the time of the revolution of 1917. My grandfather returned home to his family to work in the fields, plowing and seeding.

My father, twenty-one years old at the time the Ukrainian state was established in 1917, was aware of the meaning of the revolution in Russia, and the desire of Ukrainians to separate and declare their independence as the Ukrainian National (People's) Republic. The Ukrainian government was established and ultimately headed by Symon Petliura, who was also Chief of Military Forces, the Ukrainian National Army (UNA).

---

[1] This and the following sections are told in the voice of Wasyl Kushnir, based on his manuscript, deciphered and edited by Andrei Kushnir.

L to R: 1. My father, Andrei Semenovych Kushnir, 1896–1944. Unknown date and photographer. 2. Symon Petliura, Head of the Directorate of Ukrainian National Republic, Chief of Military Forces of Ukrainian National Army. Unknown date and photographer. Image in the United States Public Domain. Wikimedia Commons.

My father joined a section of the UNA. He took active part in battles with the advancing Russian Bolshevik forces which sought to occupy Ukrainian lands. He fought until the retreat of the crushed UNA. Eventually, in the autumn of 1919, the remaining forces crossed the border into Poland, where the Poles disarmed the soldiers and took them into captivity behind barbed wire fences.

3. Map of Ukraine, showing the approximate location of the village of Nova Bubnivka. Sven Teschke, Paweł Marynowski, Creative Commons Attribution-Share Alike 3.0 license. Used with the authors' permission.

However, earlier that summer, when the UNA's withdrawal toward the Polish border began, my father Andrei and some of the soldiers had the opportunity to depart from the retreating portions of the UNA, as the *selo* of Nova Bubnivka was only thirty kilometers from the border of Volochysk, Poland. They stopped at my grandfather's house to spend the night and to obtain provisions. My grandfather Semen gathered food and hosted a meal to refresh the tired and hungry soldiers. Upon spending the night, the UNA soldiers left the village in a westward direction, but my father remained behind with the family.

Afterwards, on July 4, 1919, the military forces of the Russian Bolsheviks entered the village of Nova Bubnivka. The neighbors immediately told them that the Petliurist forces had spent the previous night in the Kushnir *dvir* [homestead], had slaughtered a cow, taken on food, bread, meat, and hay for their horses, and left the village. The neighbors accurately reported that my father Andrei, a Petliura follower, had remained at home, but that the entire Kushnir family had gone to their field beyond the village, about two kilometers. Two *chekist*[2] Bolsheviks departed for the field.

That day, the family had gone to work in the fields: my grandfather Semen Vasylevych, grandmother Yaryna, my father Andrei, his two brothers, Avksentij and Danylo (born in 1910, so nine years old at that time), and both of father's sisters, Domakha and Ksenia. The family was working on the field and noticed that the two *chekist* Bolsheviks had turned off on their horses and were coming straight at them. My father, seeing this, hid in the tall wheat growing in the field.

Upon arriving, the *chekist* Bolsheviks immediately asked my grandfather, "where is your son Andrei, the *Petliurivets*?" They ordered the entire family to stand on their knees, pressed a rifle to each person's head, and shot off a blank round asking each the same question. In the end, one of the *chekist* Bolsheviks pressed the barrel of his rifle to the chest of my grandfather and shot, killing him in front of the entire family. My grandfather was forty-eight years old. The *chekist* Bolshevik swore and said, "go to sleep, you son-of-a-so-and-so." Then the two of them mounted their horses and left my grandfather bleeding on the ground. The family, crying and screaming, ran into the fields, out of fear.

After the *chekist* Bolsheviks left, the family returned and placed my grandfather on the wagon. Our horses took his lifeless body through the entire village to the family's homestead. There, with his body on the wagon, the horses remained grazing all night. The entire family gathered home on the second day, having spent the night in the field under the open sky, here and there, on the wheat.

After the funeral, my father remained in hiding for a long time, and, knowing that the Communist activists in the village would turn him in, he left the village. Later, the Muscovite Bolsheviks proclaimed an amnesty. It was announced that whoever served in whatever army, all was forgiven. My father returned to the village and began running the household, under the assumption that there would be no tracking down of people involved in past activities.

My father ordered, from the local stone carvers, a monument, built in four sections. On the base section was written "Here rests the body of Semen Vasylevych Kushnir, murdered by the Bolsheviks on July 4, 1919. Rest in peace, dear father."

---

[2] The *cheka* were the secret police

4. Gravestone of my Grandfather, Semen Vasylevych Kushnir, 1871–1919. Photograph by Wasyl Kushnir, September 1994.

To evidence what is written here, this photograph was taken in July 1994, when my wife Maria and I visited Ukraine. We stayed in Kyiv, in Kaniv (laying flowers at the monument to Ukrainian poet T. H. Shevchenko), and visited distant relatives in Odessa oblast. We also visited Vinnytsya, from where we hired a chauffeur who drove us to Nova Bubnivka. There we went to the cemetery where my grandfather had been buried, and found the ruins of the monument scattered in the weeds, including the lowest portion with the inscription deeply carved into the granite. I noted the place in the cemetery where my grandfather was buried. The monument was destroyed in 1930, right after the dekulakization[3] and the exile of my father to Siberia.

L to R: 5. Wasyl Kushnir, at the gravesite of Semen Vasylevych Kushnir, village of Nova Bubnivka, Ukraine, September 1994. Note the broken sections of the gravestone, destroyed by Communist activists in 1930. Photograph by Maria Kushnir. 6. Maria Kushnir, wife of Wasyl Kushnir, and Raissa Yaremchuk, cousin to Wasyl Kushnir, at the gravesite of Semen Vasylevych Kushnir, September 1994. Photograph by Wasyl Kushnir.

---

3   Soviet political repressions, including arrests, executions, and expropriation of property from better-off peasants.

After the amnesty, my father married my mother, Anna Yakivna Pidkalyuk. My mother had two brothers (Moisei [Ukrainian for Moses] and Ivan) and three sisters (Matrosia, Maryna, and Likera). My father received twenty beehives as a dowry and became a beekeeper. He increased the apiary to twenty-eight hives. Business went very well. He sold the honey in barrels, and buyers from the surrounding cities paid him good money. Usually, the buyers were Jewish businessmen, and they bought up all of the honey produced. In this family I was born on May 23, 1923.

7. My mother, Anna Yakivna Pidkalyuk Kushnir, 1902–1988. Unknown date and photographer. 8. The Kushnir family, June 20, 1930. Andrei, Wasyl, Halyna Pidkalyuk (Anna's niece, and Wasyl's cousin), Anna. Unknown photographer.

Having made some money, my father began building a fine large house on a stone foundation, roofed with terra cotta shingles. The house was completed in 1926, and the family moved there. Before that time, the family lived in my grandmother's home.

During the construction of our house, my father brought stone for the foundation with a wagon. An unfortunate accident occurred, and he broke his leg. The doctors did not properly set the bones, and his leg was shortened by four centimeters—about one and a half inches. This did not diminish his energy. My father looked after the beehives, paid off the debt for the house, and gave money to the builders for their efforts.

Dispossession and Father's Arrest

Then the misfortunes began. During the late 1920s, a time of uncertainty and lawlessness began. Agitators arrived and proclaimed that the old ways would be changed, that there would be a new way of doing things. A Polish neighbor, Budaretski, came into our house and took our bed to his house. Later, when the commune was organized, civil policemen were appointed by the commune to make arrests and confiscate property. At a village meeting, they decided to take my father's apiary for the commune. Then, my father was arrested and exiled to Siberia, my mother sent to prison as well. All their possessions were taken away and the house was converted by the authorities into a school for the *selo*. The plankwood fence that surrounded my grandmother Yaryna's house was taken apart and was used to make stables for the commune's horses.

I remember when my father was arrested. It was in May 1930, when I was seven years old. One day, a man came to our house. He said, "Kushnir, I have come to arrest you." My father asked my mother to give him a set of underwear, and one day's food. He was taken to the *selska rada*, the village council, where they locked him up with others they had arrested. It is ironic that Budaretski, the neighbor, was also arrested. Father was there for a few days, and Mother brought him food until they took him to the regional lock-up. From there, they sent him to Siberia, to a prison in Krasnoyarsk, Russia.

9. *The National Tribune*, a Ukrainian-language newspaper published in the United States, on December 6, 2009, on page 3, published a partial listing of persons of Ukrainian nationality who had been sentenced to the Steplag concentration camps by the Communist authorities during the years 1920–1950. My father's name appears near the middle of the listing on the right side of the page. Permission granted by the publisher.

> Кушнір Александр Матвеевич, 1901 г.р., ур. Львовской обл.;
> Кушнір Анастасия Филимоновна, 1926 г.р., ур. Волынской обл.;
> Кушнір Анна Николаевна, 1925 г.р., ур. Тернопольской обл.;
> Кушнір Андрей Семенович, 1889 г.р., ур. Винницкой обл.;
> Кушнір Богдан Николаевич, 1930 г.р., ур. Дрогобычской обл.;
> Кушнір Василий Спиридонович, 1924 г.р., ур. Одесской обл.;
> Кушнір Владимир Васильевич, 1932 г.р., ур. Дрогобычской обл.;
> Кушнір Владимир Иванович, 1902 г.р., ур. Винницкой обл.;

10. This list in *The National Tribune*, which includes persons whose last names began with letters from KU to LA, contains the name of my father, Andrei Semenovych Kushnir, born in 1889 in the Vinnytsya oblast. The date cited is erroneous: my father was born in 1896. Permission granted by the publisher.

But my father's imprisonment did not last long. He was given permission to visit the office of a dentist outside the prison gates. From there, he did not return to the prison, but hid in the bushes until nightfall and carefully made his way to the railway station. Coming close to the railway, he walked through the woods to avoid the station and all the police guards there, because the militia checked the documents of everyone on the platform and near the ticket windows, or waiting for a train. It was not possible to get even near the station; the militia would immediately capture and arrest the people who did not have documents.

My father had no documents. He knew that there was only one option, to walk alongside the railroad tracks through the Siberian taiga forest to the next stop on the railroad. He was without food, hungry, and fearful of attacks by wild animals. In the taiga forest, it is possible to come upon wild boars, bears, and tigers, and the only weapon he had was a stick for protection. He walked stealthily, so as not to come upon any person, along the tracks, which were surrounded by tall grass and weeds. Already very weakened, he spent the night under the open sky.

On the second day, he continued walking, further weakened and hungry, with even little hope that he would get to the next station. And here a miracle occurred—on the path, my father saw a piece of bread! He did not believe his eyes. He dropped to his knees, picked up the piece of bread and kissed it, and said a prayer to God for such a gift from the sky: on the taiga in impassable forests—a piece of bread! This was a miracle from God, said father. It raised his hopes and improved his attitude, and in this way my father spent two more days and nights fortified by this piece of bread before arriving at the next railroad station. At the station, he met a railway worker and asked when the train was coming. He also checked what guards were at the station and whether they examined documents.

It turned out that this man was a good person. He told my father when the train would arrive, and where to hide until the time the train pulled up. He told my father which railway car to choose—not one among the first cars, and not in the rear, but in the middle of the train, because the guards and the NKVD[1] were either in the front

---
[1] These initials, in Russian, stand for the People's Commissariat for Internal Affairs. This was the secret police organization, in charge of political executions, assassinations, and general repressions against all enemies of the communist system. They also administered the USSR's prisons and labor camps.

of the train or the rear. He advised my father to look, unnoticed, where the militia guards had already passed, and during the stop to get on the car where the NKVD had already checked the passengers. My father successfully used this advice.

In the railcar, my father made acquaintance with a *batyushka*, an Orthodox priest, who was travelling from the town of Chita in the lands surrounding Lake Baikal, in southern Siberia, to Moscow. This *batyushka* was a truly good person. He gladly gave my father food and money for a ticket the entire way to Moscow. In Moscow, documents again were examined by the militia and NKVD, but my father somehow avoided them.

Father was able to get to Kyiv, and there met up with mother's brother, Ivan Yakivych Pidkalyuk, who lived for a long time with his family in an apartment on 10 Solomyanka Street. Ivan Pidkalyuk had served in the Baltic naval forces and was now studying agronomy.

11. Ivan Yakivych Pidkalyuk, Anna Kushnir's brother. Unknown date and photographer.

My father's brother, Avksentij, had an apartment in the Darnytsya District, on the east bank of the Dnipro River. He helped my father find a job as a *hrushchyk*, or stevedore. There, my father broke his collarbone. After his recuperation, he obtained a job as watchman at a factory. I still possess a certificate showing his employment as a watchman at the Kyiv locomotive repair works. The document states that my father was employed continuously and received a salary of 68 *karbovantsi* 64 *kopeks*.

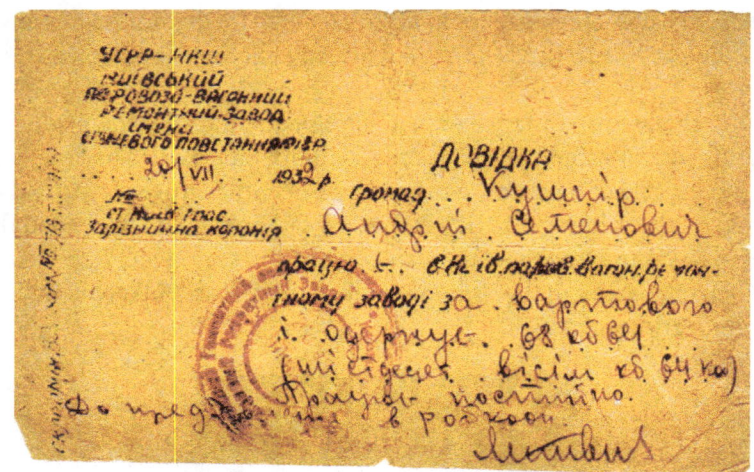

12. Father's certificate of employment.

My Mother's Travails

Now, I must provide some information about my mother, Anna Yakivna Kushnir, and her hardships after the dekulakization. After her arrest, a month after my father had been arrested, she was sent to a jail in Mariupol in southeast Ukraine. Mother also escaped from her jail, through a yard where horses were corralled. The horses were scared and started making noise. She made her way to the wire fence at the end of the corral, dug a small hole, and crawled under the wire. Unfortunately, she received many deep scratches on her back which started bleeding. She made her way to family friends in the village of Hlyadky, and then to Kyiv, to her brother, Ivan, where she joined my father. Ivan allowed both my mother and my father to live with his family.

13. My mother, Anna Yakivna Kushnir, 1931. Unknown photographer.

At that time, the government instituted obligatory issue of passports. Everyone was required to obtain a passport at the regional police station. To obtain a passport, one had to provide documents showing their social status and place of birth, as well as other documents from the *sel'rada* (short for *sel'ska rada*—the village council). Men had to show their *voennyi bilet* [military certificate], and to fill out a form with many questions, such as in which army they served during the time of the revolution. My father could not produce any documents because he served in the army of the Ukrainian National Republic, the army of Petliura. The form even had a question asking information about in which army the man's father had served (in the case of my father, Andrei, that would relate to Semen Vasylevych, his father, who had been murdered by the *chekists*).

My mother's brother, Ivan Pidkalyuk, was quite aware of my mother and father's situation. He decided to help them obtain a passport. Secretly, at night, he made a stamp from a knot in a piece of wood, created a certificate of birth, a certificate of social status, and other documents, and stamped them with the self-made stamp. It all looked formal, and the regional militia did not ask any more. With these documents my parents, after praying to God, went to the regional militia in the passport section in the Solomyanka District in Kyiv, west of the Dnipro River, and received their passports. With the passports, they were signed into the records of the regional militia, and all was in order.

As mentioned earlier, after the end of the revolution in Ukraine and Russia, the Communist government in Moscow proclaimed an amnesty to everyone who served in whatever army during the revolution of 1917–20. No one would be punished. The revolution was completed, and the Communist authorities forgave everyone. But afterwards, in the 1930s, the Bolsheviks instituted obligatory issue of passports, ordered exile and dekulakization, and the amnesty became a lie. They began arresting people, sending them to Siberian prisons, and instituting communes. They took land away from the peasants and forcefully removed people from their homes into the frost and snow, with their children and elderly people who did not want to go to the communes, or who may have said something against the Soviet authorities. They divided people into the poor, *kulaks*, and capitalists. People began telling on each other, claiming that so-and-so said something against collectivization, against the Bolsheviks. Terrible investigations began as a means to secure control over the population in Ukraine. There was instituted a "quarantine" that prevented people from going from one village to a neighboring village. People who were caught violating the quarantine were arrested and put in jail.

This is how the Soviet authorities treated the Ukrainian people. Everything the peasants had: a horse, cow, pig, calf, wagon, sled, any machinery, grinder, all was seized and taken to the commune, even plows, rakes, and everything else. Buildings, barns, sheds, and stalls for animals, all of this the village activists took away from the owners and to the commune without any compensation. Even the fences along the houses that had a fenced-in yard the activists broke apart and took to the commune. This was a real robbery of village peasants by the Communist and Bolshevik authorities, who had promised the peasants land after the end of the revolution. Instead, they took the land, all property, and everything that peasants had acquired through their labor and hard work.

In the courtyard area where mother's brother Ivan Pidkalyuk lived in Kyiv, an apartment lodging was vacated. On Ivan's recommendation, my parents obtained a nice little apartment, with two little rooms. Everything went well, and they settled in nicely. Mother and father were pleased that with all circumstances, with the help of good people and their own efforts, they could rescue themselves and begin a settled life. Until this time, there was nowhere they could turn: as father and mother said, their only choice was "from the bridge into the water." With no passport, they could not obtain work. With no passport, they could not be logged into the regional police district and could not find a place to live. Now they had passports

My mother worked a little as a seamstress, taking orders from people who lived nearby. She knew how to sew clothing and had a sewing machine that her father had given her as dowry. When the dekulakization occurred, by some miracle she was able to take the sewing machine from the house, without the head, which she had earlier taken out to my grandmother's to hide, because already the times were uncertain. When my father was sent to Siberia, mother took out various household items and distributed them among her relatives—her machine, some spools, pillows, pieces of cloth, and other items. And now, in Kyiv, this sewing machine came in handy. My father bought a manual attachment, as the machine had earlier been foot-operated. And so mother was able to make a little money for a living.

My Life After the Arrests of My Parents

After my parents were arrested and sent to exile and prison, at the age of seven I was sent to my grandmother, Yaryna. I lived with her from 1930 to 1934. My grandmother could not work, but her son Danylo Semenovych Kushnir, my uncle, worked in the commune. For some reason, they did not exile him, probably because without him, there would be no one to support my grandmother and me. My father's sister Ksenia and her husband (of Polish nationality, his last name I can't remember) were exiled. Their young son, named Saverko, was also placed in my grandmother's care. Most probably, it was another reason why my uncle Danylo was not sent away: he was the sole provider for Saverko as well. Danylo was not allowed to own much of anything, and they could not exile my grandmother, as she was from an exceptionally poor family. Under the tsar's regime, her family all worked for the *pan*, the landlord who had controlled the serfs. Now, she only had a very small house and garden, which somehow did not disturb the authorities. My grandmother was considered a very poor widow. And so in the spring, I was moved to my grandmother's house, and I went to school, which had been my father's house.

L to R: 14. My uncle, Danylo Semenovych Kushnir. Unknown date and photographer. 15. My Grandmother, Yaryna Kushnir, 1966. Unknown photographer. 16. Saverko, last name unknown, as a soldier in the Soviet army, 1947. Unknown photographer.

My recollection is that approximately seventy-five percent of the population in Nova Bubnivka was of Polish nationality and only twenty-five percent was Ukrainian. Thus, the majority of the *selo* authorities were Polish Communists, and so to mollify the Polish population during the times of 1930–31, the Soviet authorities permitted them to have their own school using the Polish language, and Polish teachers were found from the populace. I was admitted to the Polish school, but several weeks later, they threw me out, because this school was only for ethnic Poles and their children.

As a Ukrainian, I was reassigned to the school at Velyka [Greater] Bubnivka, where a Ukrainian school already existed, because the majority of population there was Ukrainian. There were three of us boys from Nova Bubnivka who went to the school at Velyka Bubnivka, about three kilometers away. We went to school every day, by foot, in summer and winter: Yuchim Lepikash, his cousin Volodymyr Lepikash, and I. Another boy, who also went a long way every day, was Stepan Bozhok from the Novy Stav village. But one or two years later, an edict was issued by the Narodnyi Komitet [People's Committee]—NARCOM [for short]—of Education prohibiting Polish schools in Ukraine, and all Polish schools were converted to schools taught in the Ukrainian language.

The Holodomor

And so came the unfortunate year of 1933, the year of Stalin's Holodomor.[1] I was ten years old, the age when children develop physically, and I had to go hungry. There was no bread. The Soviet authorities took everything. Communist activists searched our homes and sheds for foods. They searched everywhere, looking even in our kitchenware, in our pots, and in our fields, and if they found any food of any kind, everything was taken. The activists and the Komsomol [Communist party youth organization] carried long iron rods. Everywhere in our yard and in the garden, they pushed the rods into the ground to check whether someone had buried grain, potatoes, or beets. If they found any vegetables, the activists confiscated them for the commune.

17. *Daily Express* [London] headline, August 7, 1934. Public Domain, Wikimedia Commons.

---

1 For more information on the history of the Holodomor, see Ray Gamache, *Gareth Jones: Eyewitness to the Holodomor* (Cardiff: Welsh Academic Press, 2016), and Robert Conquest, *The Harvest of Sorrow: Soviet Collectivization and the Terror-Famine* (Oxford: Oxford University Press, 1987).

18. Officials on a villager's property, looking for hidden food. Photograph provided by Holodomor Research and Education Consortium, CIUS, Alberta. 19. Victims of the Holodomor in Kharkiv. Photograph provided by Holodomor Research and Education Consortium, CIUS, Alberta.

The activists took apart our barn and re-erected it on the grounds of the commune to be used as a pig sty. Property was confiscated from the so-called *kurkuls*—relatively more affluent farmers, who were exiled to Siberia in the 1930s.[2]

Every day, my uncle Danylo went to work at the commune. He was paid with raw grain: a hundred grams for a day's labor, and a measure of straw with which, in the winter, the windows could be covered. The windows were frosted in winter and covered with snow. Inside the house it was so cold that the water in our buckets was covered with ice in the morning. We washed in the evenings over the oven, where we also cooked potatoes or some soup, or baked bread, until the 1933 famine.

I remember that in early spring, when the snow had just melted, I went to the garden to find something, a potato that may have been left in the ground the previous autumn and spent the winter there. I found not a whole potato, but a piece of a potato, so white it looked like shortening. From that, my grandmother cooked a sort of soup-water. A little later, when the weeds began to grow, my grandmother steeped nettle in a kettle, a green mass. We would pull the steaming thick mass out with our hands and eat it. I climbed up on the cherry tree and ate the leaves, and when I found a lump of sap, ate that. I was always very hungry.

Later, when the wheat and the barley were starting to get grains, Saverko and I would go into the fields stealthily, so that no one could see us, and rip the green shoots and the weeds. With that, my grandmother cooked a kind of green-colored soup, very bad-tasting, with no animal fat, that we had to eat to keep from dying of hunger. Some of the neighbors would bring in their pockets a little grain, some leaves, or stalks, and my grandmother would

---

2 The Russian word for these people is *kulaks*, which is also used in English. The Kushnirs had been designated as kulaks, and thus dispossessed of their property and exiled.

cook *kasha*, a kind of cereal, or baked a *palanytsya*, a flat bread loaf, first of all for uncle Danylo, because he went to work in the commune.

Danylo would work at the commune all day and do all tasks on the same level as those who were not suffering from malnutrition. But there, certain workers had their lunch cooked in the commune kitchen, and brought to them in the field. This food was only available to the commune activists, Komsomol members and the rest of the village authorities. They were privileged to use the commune's storehouse, a gigantic and long building that housed all sorts of foodstuffs: bread, milk, cheese, butter, meat, fat, honey, fruits, and vegetables. A large portion of the food was sent to the Communist authorities in Moscow, and the rest to large cities in Russia. The government enforced quota requirements for transport of bread and other foodstuffs from Ukraine.

The head of the commune was *tovarishch*[3] Rublevskii, who later changed his name to *tovarishch* Rublev, and the head of the store was *tovarishch* Kutasevych, who always wore the keys to the commune storehouse with him. With great pride, these people held everything in their hands—all accounts in the village, and all food produce. They knew who got what: first of all, the activists, the *komnezams* and all of their kind.[4] The rest, who had not yet lost their property, could be exiled to Siberia any minute. They did not have the right to avail themselves of the commune's kitchen and had to find a means to a diminished existence, or else face famine and death from hunger.

The *kurkuls*, such as my family, were selected in 1930 for exile, first of all the men, some women and many young children. Those remaining had no means of existence. Many children died of hunger, and so did their mothers and older persons, who could not go to other villages to beg for bread, a handful of grain, or anything that anyone could give them.

I recall yet other villagers who were arrested during this time and sent to Siberia. They were our nearby neighbors, the Kurovskis, of Polish descent. They had a mill, where peasants from the entire area came to grind their grain into flour. They were also dekulaked, the mill taken over by the commune, and their house was converted to a village common area, where the authorities herded the villagers together for elections. Communist propagandists were sent from the regional administration, to lie and proclaim to the Ukrainian villages how good the Soviet authorities were for the peasants—how they gave land to the peasants and factories to the workers. No one was allowed to question, but who received the money for bread and all other farm products, and for the factory produce of the workers in the cities? The land was guarded against the peasants and never given to them for everlasting use. But a peasant who missed one day of the commune work was punished with the designation "enemy of the people" for the first offense. For being late to work, the punishment was two-months labor at some specified tasks; and for more delays, jail imprisonment for six months or longer. Commune workers were turned into slaves, and laborers who could not work for any reason were called "enemies of the socialist system."

Even if you were not a *kulak*, it was enough to say you were against the Soviet authorities and you were arrested at night and sent to a Siberian work camp. Our Polish neighbor Odzechowski, who lived across the street, was poor, had a little house, a piece of garden, two children, and a wife. He said that in serfdom days, under the master, it was better than in the commune. If peasants wanted to, they would go to work, or they would not, in which case the master would not pay them. But the master did not force anyone to work without compensation.

---

3   Literally meaning "comrade," but commonly used as a salutation or a title for Soviet citizens.
4   The *komnezams* were poor never-do-wells and petty criminals, who were given authority to rule the village in the name of Communist philosophy. These loyal people were thus empowered to rule over the dispossessed kulaks.

Immediately that night, the authorities arrested and exiled him to Siberia, and the family was left without a father. In the neighboring large village, Pakhutyntsi, fifty houses stood empty, because people had died from hunger. Hungry beggars from there came by to beg for bread or even a piece of potato.

And so, during 1932 and 1933, it was very difficult to get food. Bread could not be found in stores. Long lines formed where stores sold bread, and not everyone in line was able to obtain some. When a store opened, whatever bread was available was immediately bought up by those in front of the line, and the rest of the people would disperse—the bread was over. Again, one had to get up at night and go stand in line in front of the store. The militia protected the store, standing in the doorways and around them, to ensure that no one could enter except through the line, or that, once inside, one could not turn to another seller and purchase yet another loaf of bread, with the first loaf hidden under the arm. If a militia policeman discovered this, he would take away both loaves and push the person out of the store with no bread at all.

People sat and lay at the foot of buildings and in the streets, under bridges, swollen from hunger, mostly small children and older men of all ages, dying from hunger, so swollen that they could not walk. They died in the streets and under the bridges, and the so-called "black crow" truck picked up their bodies. Hungry people sitting on the sidewalk lifted their arms begging for a little piece of bread for their child, as people passed by sorrowfully, hungry themselves.

The greatest numbers of people died in the villages. They were driven away from their homes, or, if they were lucky enough to stay where they lived--when they died, their relatives threw the bodies into the snow, or took them out into the ravines outside the villages. Whoever was able to get to a nearby town, walked further, hungry and ragged, half-barefoot in slippers to Kyiv, with the hope that in the big city they would find bread, or at least get some by begging, first for their children, and then for themselves. This famine was artificial, created by Moscow and the Bolsheviks, because in these years, from 1931 to 1933, there was no drought, the harvests were good, but on government orders all bread was transported from Ukraine to Moscow and other cities in Russia. And the Ukrainian people were designated for starvation.

My Parents, and Their Lives During and After the Holodomor

During the famine of 1932–33, my mother, after obtaining her passport, began going by train to Russia for bread in addition to her work as a seamstress. She went whenever she had time. In Russia, bread was everywhere. So all Ukrainians who could do it went to the station and got on the trains. If there was no room inside, they crawled up on top of the cars, whether they had a ticket or not, or grabbed hold of some part of the train to get to Russia.

My mother travelled to Voronezh several times. There she could buy as much bread as she wanted, but how much bread could a woman carry? Maybe half a *pud*—eight kilograms. She could not take big bags into a railway car. On the way to Ukraine, thieves stole from people exhausted from traveling. People fell asleep from being tired and thieves did their stealing. Even when a train went slowly up a hill, thieves with hooks pulled sacks and baskets with bread from the roofs of the cars.

As I mentioned earlier, my father's brother, Avksentij, who lived in Darnytsya beyond the Dnipro River, had helped my father obtain employment as a stevedore, and then a watchman. Avksentij worked as a conductor on the Kyiv railway passenger station. During this time, Avksentij advised my father to submit an application for employment with the railway administration. With the passport and documents from a place of residence in Kyiv, my father was admitted to work as a conductor on passenger trains for local and long distance routes.

Having survived the famine of 1933, my family again faced a big misfortune! Father was assigned to accompany a high-ranking official of the Trans-Baikal Railway to the city of Vladivostok in a comfortable rail car specially outfitted for high-ranking Communists, with all accoutrements and furnishings, a reserved train with no stops between Kyiv and Vladivostok. With a female conductor, my father was to stay in the head car and to serve the important Communist official. The car was heated with coal furnaces, and it was my father's job to make sure that it was warm in the car, and that there was a sufficient supply of coal and essentials during the trip. The lady conductor had her own duties: to provide the official everything he wanted, to clean up, wash, and so forth; she was also responsible for checking the temperature inside the car.

If the important official required something, he would specify what to buy at the next station at the buffet, restaurant, or store, and gave money to father, taking a packet of twenty-ruble banknotes from the cabinet. He took out, behind my father's back, a whole packet of money and held it out as though he didn't see how much he gave, only asking, "Andrei, will it be enough for you to go to the buffet during our next stop and to buy me some smoked fat, a half kilogram, and a bottle of spirits? Here, this is for you, maybe it isn't enough?" He would not take back the change.

And so they travelled from Kyiv to Moscow to Chita, but during their journey the official liked to leave the car at some stops and go into the station buildings to use the telephone for business or otherwise. He would always say, "Andrei, I am going into the station, you watch the car," and father would always answer, "Yes, *tovarishch* minister, everything will be in order."

There were no incidents, until one time, somewhere past Krasnoyarsk at a large train station, the official left the car and did not say he was going into the station. Of course, the conductor's duty is to always check the train's door to make sure it is closed properly with the key. Father went to check the door, and since it was open, locked it with the key, and went to the compartment designated for the conductor. When the official left the car, unnoticed, the train began moving, and the official was barely able to grab hold of the metal handles outside the train door. Since the train was moving fast, his banging was not heard inside the train. This was a winter trip, and in Siberia the temperatures fall severely, down to fifty degrees Celsius below zero. Father told me that if you spit, your spit would immediately freeze and hit the ground as a chunk of ice. The official was not dressed warmly and became very sick later.

Now, the conductors—that is, my father and the female conductor—noticed that the official was not in the train. So where was he? They heard the weak banging on the door. Father dashed to the door, and there was the official, barely alive and blue from the cold. Livid with anger, the official jumped at my father, angrily screaming, "I will have you shot! Why was the door locked with key, you should have looked for me first!" "But *tovarishch* minister," said my father, "you did not tell anyone that you went into the station. Our duty is to lock the door with the key when the train begins to move." The official began running around the train car. He yelled to the female conductor, "Give me alcohol," and told her to rub him down with the alcohol, as he was feeling very ill. He started coughing and got a high temperature. How did he nurse himself from this illness? At the major train stops, doctors visited him and gave him medical assistance. And so the train travelled to Chita, which is near the deepest lake in the world, Lake Baikal.

The official dismissed my father from his service duties and provided him with a paper from the Chita-Moscow-Kyiv railway as a proof for the NKVD that he had a legitimate reason to make his journey back. At that time, the NKVD checked the passengers riding on the trains, asking for their destination and the reason of their journey. Everyone was to have a passport and other documents. The official gave my father a free pass for the train to Kyiv. As for the official himself, he said he would stop in Chita for two or three weeks, and then travel to Vladivostok per his assignment.

During this time, in Kyiv, the NKVD came to the apartment, to mother, knocking on the door. Mother was at home, and the NKVD officer asked "Are you Anna Kushnir?" Mother, seeing the uniforms, realized that they came to arrest them both, and answered, "No, no one is home. I am a neighbor and have keys to watch over the apartment. From time to time, I also water the plants, but I am not certain when they will be home." The NKVD officer said, "They must be in hiding. We will find them." Mother waited several days, to discern at least why the NKVD was searching for them. Then, she went to the regional station of the NKVD, pretending to be a neighbor, to make sure that she would not be blamed for anything. The officer on duty told her to "go home, citizen, we have a warrant for them, they are dispossessed *kulaks*, have been exiled, and have bought passports for gold. We know where he works, so do not worry." Her brother Ivan's wife, Aleksandra, learned from neighbors that a woman had arrived, by the name of Seklita, from Nova Bubnivka, and had seen my mother and father. She went to the NKVD, where she testified that she knew the Kushnirs, and that she positively identified them. She also told that they had been dekulaked and sent to Siberia.

This was no joke, then. Now my mother now knew exactly why the NKVD was asking after them. Mother did not go back to the apartment to spend the night—she went to the train depot, to the dispatcher, and asked whether he knew when Kushnir was returning from his assignment in the Far East. In the dispatcher's office they already knew, as the office head had called the city of Chita, that conductor Kushnir had been relieved and would soon be returning to Kyiv from his assignment. They also knew that the NKVD was searching for him. At the office, they asked who she was, but mother said again that she was a neighbor, and that she wanted to know because she received word that the Kushnirs were to appear at the regional NKVD.

From that time, every day, my mother came to the Kyiv station to meet father. When she saw him coming on the train from Moscow, she immediately told him not to go home, as the NKVD was waiting for him there and they wanted to arrest them both. Mother explained the situation to him, and they spent two nights in the station depot on the benches. Mother decided to buy tickets to the Odessa oblast, to the town of Try Krynytsi [the name translates into English as Three Wells], where Halyna Besarab, the daughter of her brother Moisei, lived. Halyna was the girl in the photograph of the Kushnir family taken in June, 1930.[1] She had married Vasyl Besarab and now lived near Odessa. The Kushnirs would try to find a better life there and perhaps hide from the NKVD, and mother might somehow obtain a job, whatever might come by.

20. Halyna and Vasyl Besarab, 1965. Unknown photographer.

---
1   See Image 8 above.

Unfortunately, the old troubles would arise in the Odessa region—first, let us see your passport, stamped with the place of your residence. Immediately, you are asked to go before the regional section of the militia, which was to stamp the passport to document that you had legal grounds to be here during this period. They would ask, "Why are you here?" Everyone wants to go to Kyiv, and you are coming from Kyiv—this is very suspicious. Then, you must have a certificate from your place of employment. All your papers would be verified. Only if everything went well, and father found a job, only then they would have the right to live in the new place. And so, there were no apparent possibilities for resettling in the Odessa oblast. My parents spent three weeks with Halyna and her husband, Wasyl, hidden from neighbors so that no one would see them and no suspicion would be raised.

Late one evening, they went to the Try Krynytsi train station to spend the night until morning, when the train for Kyiv arrived. Again, on the bench at a train station, in a troubled, relentless world, with nowhere to turn, nowhere to hide, they both fell asleep. A thief, noticing two people who had fallen asleep on the bench, came up to my father and quietly put his hand into his inside breast pocket. He took out the money, passport, and other documents that father had with him. Father felt the presence of the evil-souled thief over him, jumped to his feet, grabbing at his own chest. The thief also jumped back, frightened, and asked father, "Why are you scared, I'm not touching you." After such a scare, my parents did not close their eyes until morning when they boarded the train to Kyiv. They arrived in Kyiv late at night, and went to my mother's brother, Ivan Pidkalyuk, told him all about their misfortunes, about their journey to the Odessa region, still in fear, and without any plans. They would wander about Kyiv during the day, and late in the evening they would come unnoticed to Uncle Ivan, or sometimes to father's brother Avksentij in Darnytsya, on the other side of the Dnipro River. And so it went for three weeks. My father was very sad that he had to give up his work as a conductor. He loved travelling by train on the near and far railway routes in Ukraine.

Time passed since he left that job, filled with the trip to the Odessa region and the unproductive wanderings around the Kyiv streets and bazaars. It was a hopeless situation. Father travelled to the Svyatoshynskyi district by tram No. 6, to the fourth stop, the very end of the tram line. There begins the *selo* of Bilychi, a corner half-settled by local peasants and workers from nearby Kyiv factories. He asked about an apartment right at the very end of Bilychi, and surprisingly, my parents were able to rent a single room from a man named Mykola Vasylenko for thirty rubles per month.

Three months passed and no one asked questions, but to gain employment, they would need to show their passports and papers to the regional militia in Svyatoshynsky. The passport my father had showed that its owner was registered with the Solomyanskyi district militia, and bore a stamped seal. It was necessary to take the risk, summon the courage to go to the Svyatoshynskyi district militia and try to see what they would say, and God would provide. In the district militia, the officer in charge, whose job was to handle registrations in passports, asked, "But do you have a job?" and father said yes, he could bring documentation in three weeks. The officer in charge asked my father to leave his passport and explained that he would see to it that the evidence from the Solomyanskyi section of the militia would be received. Only then he would enter my father into the Svyatoshynskyi district. Immediately, in the presence of my father, he telephoned and spoke with the officer in charge at the Solomyanskyi district militia. He told my father that next day, all would be taken care of. No one had evidently checked, or provided information. This militia officer in charge apparently was a person sent from God himself, said my father. On the second day, my father received his passport with a new stamp, indicating his registration in Bilychi.

I Rejoin My Parents

Father found a job at the train park named after Lenin, as a conductor for passenger trains in Kyiv. Everything now seemed fine; father worked as a conductor, mother began to sew clothes for her neighbors, and in 1934 my parents took me back from my grandmother in Nova Bubnivka, where I had lived since they had been first arrested in 1930. My uncle Danylo brought me to my parents in Bilychi, and I continued my education at the Bilychi sub-middle school, where I completed the seventh year of instruction.

L to R: 21. First class of Bilychi sub-middle school, 1931–38. Wasyl Kushnir's photo is in the bottom middle. Unknown photographer. 22. A close-up of Wasyl Kushnir in the school photo.

Uncle Danylo

I now turn to the year 1937. In Nova Bubnivka, where he lived with my grandmother Yaryna, my uncle Danylo Semenovych Kushnir was arrested by the NKVD. My grandmother said that at night a "black raven" car arrived, and the door to her house thundered. Dressed only in his night shirt, uncle Danylo opened the door, not knowing who was knocking. Immediately, he was arrested. He was not even allowed to put on any warmer clothing. They drove him into the town of Chornyi Ostriv [translates into English as Black Island], and there they savagely beat him on his head and elsewhere with a revolver, asking what my uncle knew about conspiracies against the Communist government in Ukraine. Uncle Danylo worked honestly in the commune and did nothing against the Communist government. He had never said anything against anyone. Based on the NKVD's false accusations, forged so that they could forcefully send people for slave labor in Siberia, anyone could be arrested as an "enemy of the Soviet authorities" and forced to sign confessions against himself, as though he really did commit some offense to destroy the Soviet authorities in Ukraine. During the interrogations, the NKVD beat people horrendously, put their fingers in the doorway and slammed the door, broke their bones, and exhorted confessions to be signed. Finally, when the prisoners were physically broken by the torture, they signed the confession, and the three (there were always three) judges meted out the punishment of exile in concentration camps in Siberia.

Uncle Danylo spent several months in the jail in Vinnytsya, until the NKVD gathered many others, brought them in a freight train with barred windows and with locked doors, and carried them away to suffer their punishment, each of them sentenced by three NKVD judges. Some received sentences of ten years, others, fifteen or twenty years of heavy labor behind barbed wire in unheated barracks, which they were required to build themselves. Each day, under guard, they were sent to work to clear the forests. They also performed all other kinds of heavy labor. They were given bad food, with very little bread, and each person received only a small amount. Only people who met the quota got a full portion; otherwise, they only received a half portion. Many became sick from insufficient and poor food. Forced to work, the sick people died from starvation and the cold.

The prison train that carried my uncle Danylo went for three days without opening the doors in the cars. Only on the third day, the doors were opened and a pail of cold water and one loaf of bread given for every two people. Then the doors were shut, and the train continued onward. Ill and weak people did not receive any medical assistance. And so the train continued until they reached the town of Chita, and from there they were escorted to a concentration camp at the Mongolian border, where each day they were led to work under the control of armed guards to build bunkers on the borders of the USSR as fortification against the Japanese.

I learned this information from my uncle Danylo's correspondence, probably less than six letters or postcards. When the bunkers were completed, the entire concentration camp in the town of Chita was moved by freight cars from Chita, through Moscow, to the north, to the city of Arkhangelsk. There, everyone was transferred to a ship and taken through the White Sea and the North Sea, past the islands of Novaya Zemlya [translates into English as New Land], then by steamship to the mouth of the river Yenisei, and eight hundred kilometers down the river, where they were unloaded in the snow forest.

Many died during the journey, and those who arrived alive were put behind barbed wire and forced to build their own barracks, from which they were driven on foot each day, under force, to work, building bridges over the Yenisei River. Only snow forest could survive in this area. The ground was frozen nine months of the year. Only during the remaining three months the river was navigable, and a steamship brought food for the concentration camp.

The food was rotten cabbage and flour riddled with worms. People died from hunger and severe freezing temperatures, got sick from diseases, got *tsynha* [scurvy], and their teeth fell out due to vitamin deficiencies. Every day, dead people were carried from the barracks. There were no funerals. The bodies were thrown behind the camp, and wild animals tore them apart. The concentration camp was surrounded with barbed wire and guards with weapons watched so that no one could escape.

I saved the last postcard received from my uncle Danylo. Addressed to my father, it was written on June 1, 1941. We received it right before the beginning of the Second World War. In those days we all lived in Bilychi. The address of the concentration camp is clearly written: "Komi SSR, City of Abez, Camp Mail Post no. 274, Usynskii Stroimost [Usynskii Bridge Construction]."

23. Postcard from my uncle, Danylo Kushnir, dated June 1, 1941, front.

24. Postcard from my uncle, Danylo Kushnir, dated June 1, 1941, back side.

This card is now very old and worn, but still I keep it. It says:

June 1, 1941. Good health to you, dear family. I am informing you that I am alive and well, finding myself at the old place and that I am not receiving letters from anyone. I have received four letters, to which I have responded. Here, it is already spring. The ground is unfreezing. Soon, passenger steamships will arrive, and the mail will come more regularly. I send you all a deep bow: you little brother Andrei, B. Anna, sister Domka; and I send greetings to Vasya, Volodymyr and all the other wonderful people. I beg you to write letters and to tell me all the news about mother's health and about everything else. I live [unintelligible], but here the climate is extremely damp and cold, a great [unintelligible] has caused my health to deteriorate. Let mother know about me because I do not have paper to write her a letter. Goodbye, dear family. I will leave from here on July 1, 41. D. Kushnir.

There, in the concentration camp, my uncle Danylo suffered the inhospitable climate of the northern regions, with their horrifying cold, where even the vegetation is stunted in growth. Uncle Danylo wrote that he could not even chop a piece of wood for a wagon axle, because trees did not grow that tall in the taiga. His postal cards provide proof and objective evidences to my recollection of the tragic years of repressions carried through by the Communist regime of the authoritarian Moscow government.

After the independent Ukrainian state was established, my son, Andrei, tried to obtain more information about the ultimate fate of my uncle Danylo. After various contacts with the Ukrainian Department of Security Services and the authorities of the Khmelnytskyi region, on May 15, 2012, he received a letter from the regional State Archives, stating that my uncle Danylo was arrested on November 5, 1937 for violating statute 54–10 of the Ukrainian USSR law against counterrevolutionary activities, that he was not married, that on November 16, 1937 he was sentenced by three NKVD workers to ten years at a correctional labor facility, and that no further information was available. The letter stated that on August 16, 1989, at the recommendation of the Khmelnytskyi region prosecutors, he was rehabilitated. While more information may exist in Russia, which holds the records of the Soviet Union, we have not contacted the hostile government in Moscow. A letter sent to the Republic of Komi in 2014 with a request for information about my uncle brought no reply.

Україна Хмельницька обласна державна адміністрація **Державний архів** **Хмельницької області** 29000, м.Хмельницький, вул.Грушевського, 99 тел. 76-47-39, факс 76-47-39	**Ukraine** **Khmelnitsky regional state** **administration** **State archives** **Khmelnitsky region** 29000 Khmelnitsky, 99 Grushevsky st. Phones: 76-47-39, fax: 76-74-39

№ 130/К-01-15   от 15.05.2012

Кушнир А.В.
США

АРХИВНАЯ СПРАВКА

Гр. КУШНИР Даниил Семенович 1910 года рождения, украинец по национальности, уроженец и житель с. Ново-Бубновка (теперь с.Бубновка) Черноостровского (с 1962 года — Виньковецкого) района Каменец-Подольской (с 1954 года — Хмельницкой) области, был арестован 5 ноября 1937 года Черноостровским районным отделом НКВД по обвинению по ст.54-10 УК УССР в контрреволюционной деятельности.

На день ареста в браке не состоял.

Решением особой тройки УНКВД по Каменец-Подольской области от 16 ноября 1937 года гр. Кушнир Д.С. был осужден к десяти годам лишения свободы в исправительно-трудовом лагере. Дальнейшая его судьба неизвестна..

На основании заключения прокуратуры Хмельницкой области от 16 августа 1989 года гр. Кушнир Д.С. реабилитирован.

Основание: ФР-6193, оп.12, д.П-19862, л.1,5,21,22,24,42.

Заместитель директора архива   С.Р.Михайлова

Начальник отдела информации
и использования документов   Н.А.Кузьмина

Мыськова 797559

25. Letter dated May 15, 2012 to Andrei Kushnir, USA, from the State Archives, Khmelnytskyi Region, Khmelnytskyi Regional State Administration.

Life with My Parents in Bilychi

When we lived in Bilychi, I made a pair of skis. I soaked some long, flat boards, and bent them where they should be bent, and went skiing with my friends. They all had store-bought skis, but mine were adequate. One day, we were skiing down a hill with a frozen pond below. I skied over the pond, and the ice, still thin, cracked under me. I went down up to my neck in the water. When I got out, I walked the three kilometers to our home. Later that day, I became very ill. I had a high temperature, and very bad catarrh, combined with a kidney malfunction. My parents took me to a clinic, where a Jewish female doctor prescribed a very severe diet—absolutely nothing spicy, salty, or vinegary—only water, milk, white bread, and dextrose—and nothing cold. That doctor saved my life. When we came back home, my parents watched over me as I lay so sick, but I recovered. Since that time, I have had kidney problems, such as stones. I still do not drink anything cold, and have only been really comfortable with bland food since my illness.

Before I finished the seventh grade, a memorable episode occurred during the New Year holidays. My father and I sometimes went to a church in Kyiv located near the Baikov cemetery. My parents were deeply religious: they believed in God and loved their Orthodox Church. Three or four times a year, they would go to church, usually during the Christmas holidays, at New Year, and Easter. I often accompanied my father. We did not notice that from the Pioneer organization of the Bilychi school, the activist komsomol sent spies to the Baikov cemetery to see if any of the students went to church and if so, who exactly was there. These spies noticed my father and me in church, and drew a caricature, which they hung on the school newsboard in the corridor:

26. "Wasyl Kushnir, churchgoer, goes to pray at the Baikov cemetery in Kyiv." Facsimile drawing by Wasyl Kushnir.

For me, this brought a denigration and shaming among my fellow students. Most of them greeted me with a smirk. I lowered my head to my desk and wept quietly with this embarrassment. A fellow student, Sonia Kovalenko, noticed this. She came up to me and asked why I was crying. She said that she also went to church, that others could laugh if it was funny to them. This gave me a little courage, but at the same time I understood that I could not continue my education at that place.

L to R: 27. Wasyl Kushnir. Unknown date and photographer. 28. Wasyl Kushnir and father, Andrei Kushnir, May 5, 1937. Unknown photographer. 29. Wasyl Kushnir, 1938. Unknown photographer.

The applications for the next level of schooling required additional documents, my birth certificate, paperwork from the prior school, and other documents about my parents. The application also included a question about the birth date of my father, who was born in 1896. There were more questions that had to be answered in detail, questions that caused my father to tell me to start looking for work, because there was no path for further education in the schools. It would not be safe for us to answer all those questions. Indeed, when I attempted to apply to the FZU [*Fabrichno-zavodskoe uchilishche*], a trade school, I was required to write an affidavit and provide proper documents, so this path was closed for me as well. It was not possible to continue with any kind of education. I never made an application to the komsomol organization, because I wanted to escape their questions.

Finally, I got a job in a sewing factory named after Maxim Gorky, in the Demievtsi [later renamed Stalinka] neighborhood in Kyiv, as an assistant mechanic for sewing machines. The factory employed mostly women. We only had two men—myself and the sewing section master, who taught me how to repair the machines. Every day I had to take the tram No. 6 from the fourth transfer station. At the Bilshovyk [Bolshevik] station I took the Pullman tram No. 7. The Pullman cars were very long, with the entrance in the middle. From there, I went to to Besarabka-Khreshchatyk station and took the tram No. 18 to Stalinka, to the factory, to my job. It was a long route, but I took it every day. We hoped that maybe everything would change and I would find another job. However, I worked at the factory until the beginning of the Second World War in 1941.

The son of our then-landlord in Bilychi, Yukhim Mnishchenko, received a summons from the military draft office. He was healthy enough to serve, and should have gone, but my father advised him and his father to turn their attention to the corn in their garden. Where would the boy go? The Germans had already surrounded Kyiv.

Our landlord understood and hid his son from the war. Yukhim called several neighbors, pretending that he was going to the voenkomat, but that evening he came home quietly.

In those days, some people in Bilychi kept a cow or pig. Mnishchenko dug out a large hole in the yard, near the place where his cow stood. He lined the walls and floor with straw, and hid his son there the entire time until the Germans entered Kyiv. Kyiv was surrounded by Germans for seventy-two days. The landlord was very afraid, and said that if the NKVD would catch the boy, he would be immediately executed for desertion.

We all knew this, but everyone was waiting for the arrival of the Germans, and believed that the Bolsheviks would never return. Many local people were waiting for a regime change, not aware that the Fascist Germans would, just as the Communists, bring the yoke of slavery upon our people and disregard our basic human rights, as soon as they drove away the Muscovite Communists. The local population greeted the Germans with bread and salt, and flowers as well, hoping that finally there would be the end of firing squad executions of innocent people, including Ukrainian peasants, who honestly worked in the communes, and the workers, who gave their sweat and blood to carry out the five-year plans in four years, the horrifying goals being met at one hundred percent and one hundred and fifty percent, and more, for miserable pay, and the ubiquitous queues for all everyday items, for clothes, shoes, coal, and kerosene to light the lamps in their village homes.

There was virtually no electricity in the villages. Most people lit their houses with kerosene lamps. As mentioned above, the commune workers were paid for a day's labor: they received 100 grams of raw grain or 200 grams of rye or raw wheat and a measure of straw in the winter to burn in the home oven. The oven was used to cook food, bake bread, and in the winter season it would heat the living space (slightly). When the winter was very cold, and there was not much straw, one had to go to the *sel'rada* and beg the head of the commune for more straw, because in the house the water froze, and the children were coughing from the cold. The head of the commune would call the brigadier and tell him to bring some straw. Such was the life.

This Communist leadership of the Moscow Bolsheviks in Ukraine brought the exile to Siberia and other grave hardships, for whatever reason. They would apply the labels "enemy of the people," "nationalist," "agent of a foreign power" to the few who returned from prison or Siberian exile.

The German Army Enters Kyiv

This episode occurred just as the Germans entered Kyiv. The month of June brings rather hot weather in Ukraine, and already I slept not in the house, but outside behind the animal barn. There, the landlord allowed us to stack wood, which my father and I brought from the nearby forest to heat our apartment in winter, a bundle of dry branches each. In the apartment, we had a stove, which heated the room, and a kitchen hot plate on which mother cooked borsch, or fried potatoes, and even heated water to do the laundry. One night, I went outside to sleep on this woodpile. I had a little mattress that I made from reeds and when the weather was clear, it was almost comfortable. All at once, I awoke to a terrible roar and sound of airplanes, not knowing that these were the German bombers flying over the 43rd aviation factory which manufactured Soviet warplanes and motors. I could not sleep until dawn and did not know what had occurred. In the morning, radio reports and posted signs proclaimed that Fascist Germany had attacked, breaking its treaty with the Soviet Union, that victory would be ours and the enemy would be defeated. At this point, all was clear: the 43rd military factory, the factory Bilshovyk, and other important targets were bombed.

As usual, I got ready to go to work, and when I arrived at the fourth transfer station, I squeezed into the last car of the tram, which was overfull of people going to work. The people in the tram were all talking about the attack of the German airplanes. I, too, began talking about the explosions I heard in the night, until someone tapped me on the shoulder and, waving his finger in warning, said, "Young man, what do you do, you and I will go to the police station when the tram stops." The police station was right on the second transfer station, the next tram stop. I quickly understood that I was now in trouble. When the tram stopped, I squeezed low under people's legs, jumped out of that car, and ran up to the front car, exhaling all my breath to squeeze in. Thus I got to the place where I worked. At work, everyone received gasmasks to be ready for war. Thereafter, I stopped going to work there.

When the Germans were taking over Kyiv, two shells from their parade fell in our neighbor's kitchen garden. They didn't cause any harm, but they marked the Germans' entrance. On the Zhytomyrskyi express road they marched in columns on parade. No one shot at them, and they didn't shoot at anyone. On the express road in Bilychi and further in Sviatoshyno, where the Ukrainian residents came out to see the German army, the Ukrainians placed a large table and covered it with embroidered tablecloths, with a loaf of bread and salt. When a column of German soldiers paused by the table, a group of Ukrainian enthusiasts greeted the German soldiers, began hugging the soldiers and expressed their joy at the liberation of Ukraine from the Communist "Heaven," or rather, Terror, with the hopes of a better life in Ukraine, the center of all countries in Europe.

Before the entrance of the foremost German troops, a new iron bridge on the Zhytomyrskyi express road was blown up where it crossed the tramway line, but it did not delay the Germans from going forward into the center of Kyiv. My father and I went to see what this explosion on the road was. When we arrived at the new bridge, where the Soviet army had placed mines, we saw that the bridge had been totally destroyed, but the German army went around underneath it. Then, they drove and marched all the way to the Bilshovyk factory, until they met iron obstructions called *rohatky* and could not march or drive further. Father and I walked, on this same road, beneath the chestnut trees, to get back to Bilychi. We were caught by a German officer, who beckoned with his finger to come towards him. Father and I walked up to the officer and my father, who didn't know the German language at all, started talking to the German in Ukrainian: "My son is not a Communist, look, he has a cross on his neck, and I have a cross on my neck." The officer grabbed me by the shirt and pushed my chest so hard that I fell to the ground. Father became afraid and said to me, "Let's go more quickly from here, this is the frontline, the Germans can kill us, and who will ask questions?" And so, my father and I hurried, so that no one would see us. We returned to Bilychi.

We did not know yet what the new German regime would bring, but already it became apparent that the Germans did not bring any relief to the people. The communes were left alone; the local Communists were also not investigated. All Communists were left in their places, wondering about their fate, because the German substitute authorities needed their advice. The authorities began taking people to Germany for slave labor, choosing whomever the head of the commune designated.

Return to Nova Bubnivka

On the third day of German occupation, my father and I decided to leave Bilychi and, taking some food for the road, return on foot to our village of Nova Bubnivka, Chornyi Ostriv district, Vinnytsya region. The village of Nova Bubnivka is over 450 kilometers or about 280 miles away from Kyiv by railroad. Mother was left alone in the apartment of the Mnishchenkos in Bilychi. Father carried a folding metal bed that he had earlier bought for me for ten rubles at a bazar. Coming out of Bilychi, we took the direction toward Fastiv, in the western direction from Kyiv, next to the train tracks. The train tracks were not narrowed from the wider rails of the Soviet Union to the narrower Western rails. Father walked first, and I behind him on the tracks, in case there were mines. My father took the risk on himself, to protect me with his own body. We knew that the Soviets had planted mines, and as we walked along the railway tracks we saw the bodies of local residents who had been blown up.

So my father and I walked a hundred kilometers to the Fastiv city station, where we spent the night with some good people. They fed us and also administered to our medical needs, because this trek left blisters on our feet and under our toes, making it impossible to continue. They had to puncture the blisters with a needle and white thread, and overnight, the water in the blisters ran out, the blisters somewhat healed, and it was possible to walk further. And so my father and I walked another forty-five kilometers on the second day to a place where the gauge of the railway tracks changed and the train went to the Proskuriv station. This city is now named Khmelnytskyi. And so, following the advice of a helpful railroad switchman, we were able to find an empty rail car that was going to that city. From there it was not far to Nova Bubnivka, another forty-five kilometers and we were home. There, we were surprised to encounter my grandmother, Yaryna, my father's mother. She still lived in her old house, where the windows were only a foot higher than the ground. Grandmother Yaryna was very happy with our return. We could not enter the house my father built, as it had been converted into the village school with desks, benches, and bookcases. When we arrived at Nova Bubnivka, we found out from the newspaper that when the Germans were already in Kyiv, the Soviets mined Khreshchatyk, the most important street in the city. The Soviets secretly destroyed the best and the oldest section of Khreshchatyk, so that not only did many Germans and civilians die, but the center of the capital city of Ukraine suffered criminal destruction, deliberately carried out by Moscow.

After a week's time, my father travelled to Kyiv to bring back my mother, who had remained in the village of Bilychi. They packed their few belongings, and with the help of the neighbors they took them to the train station in Kyiv. There, they found a train that left with empty cars to the west in the direction of Proskuriv, and with great difficulty they arrived at Nova Bubnivka. Again, the village council did not allow us to enter our house. They told us to go to the *Gebietskommissar*, an area commissioner installed by the Germans, to obtain permission. If the German authorities allowed it, we could enter our house.

My father travelled to the town of Proskuriv to the German *Gebietskommissar*, who listened intently to his translated story. Father told him we had been dispossessed and sent to Siberia, and now we returned to our village and wanted to take our house back and live in it. The German answered that since it was wartime, the German authorities had no time to devote to civilian matters, and so my father would have to wait. When the war ended, all property rights would be determined.

My father went to the meeting of the village council authorities, but no one was sure what to do with him. Apparently, unofficially, the head of the village said, "Kushnir, we know that this was your house and you built it, so at our own risk you can enter this house." With that, my father returned, and at our own risk, we settled into our house. Father asked for help because grandmother was old and infirm. The village council helped us a little bit, they let us take a little food, some flour for bread, five kilograms of butter and some two liters of milk a day from the commune's store. This was our sole support. Grandmother had a small kitchen garden, with potatoes and some vegetables, but it was far from enough for four people.

We undertook to rebuild the inside of the house. The village council did not say anything to my father because he was an invalid. As I recounted earlier, he had broken his leg, and the doctor did not reset it properly, so that the bones did not grow together well. That leg was four centimeters shorter than the other, and father always limped to one side. We took out all of the school furniture, and the village council kept those items. Other things were built to return the house to its original appearance: we added the oven, installed the house heating, moved several walls, and the house was converted back to living quarters for a family. I slept on the metal bed that my father had carried all the way from Bilychi, and mother and father slept on planks placed over two sawhorses, on a mattress filled with straw. They told me to go work in the commune. Every day I went to plow the fields with horses, while my mother and father took care of the property. Father went to the district orchard and purchased many fruit trees—apples, pears, cherries, plums, and others. We planted the new trees outside the house.

By the end of 1942, the Germans decided to restructure the *sel'rada*. They also conscripted young men to watch over the railway line. Every evening we had to walk out to the railway station in the town of Narkevych, which was about ten kilometers away from us. The railway was guarded by Hungarian soldiers. But we civilian young men (I was nineteen years old) were twice every night forced to patrol from one end to the other, some two or three kilometers, on the railway tracks, watching for partisans. Clearly, we were treated as hostages. While we carried no weapons, the Hungarian soldiers checked us and gave us the password, a different one each night. In the morning, we were dismissed and went back to our homes. It was fortunate that we did not see any partisans and did not get into any incidents, where we could have been shot by one side or the other. We received no compensation for this. From the autumn of 1942, every evening, eleven or twelve young men from our *selo* Nova Bubnivka walked the watch over the railway, until April 1943.

Conscription to Forced Labor in Germany

The *sel'rada* was forced by the Germans to designate for work in Germany as many people from the village as possible. They were to appear before a commission in the district city of Chornyi Ostriv.

A messenger from the village council brought a notice that I was chosen for forced departure to Germany and had to appear at the collection point in Chornyi Ostriv for a medical examination by the German commandant. I could only bring necessary things, such as clothes, and food only for a couple of days. A month earlier, my mother was also chosen for work in Germany, but at the medical examination she was not accepted because of her age. Only younger people were taken.

On April 17, 1943, a group of fifteen or eighteen young men (I don't recall exactly how many), including me, appeared before the German commission, which looked us over and immediately made us board a freight train. We all settled down on the floor of the cars. The doors were not closed. At the collection point, it had been emphasized, through a translator, that no one should think of running away because in the last car there were armed German guards. From Chornyi Ostriv, in the westward direction, the train passed two stations, Narkevych and Vitivtai. Then it came to a stop, and a young man jumped from the train and began running away from his car. He was killed with two shots. The train stopped completely, and a German soldier with a translator walked through the entire train warning not to run, and threatening to kill us if we did. All who sat in the doorways of the cars saw the body of the killed boy lying several meters from the train, and all understood that they should not try to escape.

Our transport came to the border of Poland, went through Poland, and arrived at the German border near the town of Peremyshl. There all were moved from the train into barracks for medical examinations and disinfection. We were examined by German medical specialists, were all required to put our clothes through a heater that killed bacteria and to bathe, and then we were separated into groups, depending on where we were to work. Our train car and several neighboring cars, about one hundred and fifty persons in total, were sent to a camp in the town of Wiesengrund, in district of Mies, Sudetengau. Others were sent to large farms.

At the border of Germany, girls and women were driven to separate barracks. Boys and men were sent to a camp right away, overseen constantly by a *Lagerführer*. A few days later they gave us all uniforms: light brown shirt, jacket, and trousers. We also received *Holzschuhe*, clogs with half-inch-thick wooden soles and patches to sew on our sleeves, designating Eastern workers—*Ostarbeiter*, or OST, as our patches stated.

30. Drawing of an OST patch by Wasyl Kushnir.

These patches were only for *Ausländer* [non-Germans] who came from the Soviet Union. The Ukrainians from Polish-dominated Galicia did not receive the OST designation. Instead, they received documentation, a certificate, a sort of a passport, and coupons for food. They were regarded as Europeans under Polish occupation. Poles had to wear a patch with a "P" on their left sleeves, but they received coupons for food and they could buy everything they wanted in stores. They were assigned to work for farmers in the villages. Slovaks, Czechs, and the French had designated construction and mining positions.

Almost all people taken from our village were sent to the town of Wiesengrund in Sudetengau, an area of Czechoslovakia taken over by Germany. The town housed Messerschmitt plane factories, which had been already bombed. When the allies began massive bomber flights, the military armaments were always the first targets. These places saw the most destruction, and we just started to cover over the bomb craters. This did not last long; afterwards, we began repairing terra cotta roofs on houses that had been hit by the bombing. Soviet prisoners of war made and baked the tiles and laid them out, and we stood on a ladder and handed them from one to the other all the way from the trucks to the roof, and climbed to cover the roofs. We lived in stables that also housed horses; however, everything was clean. We slept on double-deck wooden bunk beds. Each day, the Germans brought us food: in the morning ersatz coffee, a small loaf of bread, and a stick of margarine for ten men. These we divided between ourselves. For lunch there was turnip soup, and dinner also included bread and some kind of cereal. It was poor food and hard work. The city of Wiesengrund also had barracks for military and administration personnel, but already it all stood empty, except for about a hundred men who looked after the stables and kept order for everyone who lived there. The barracks and administrative buildings were surrounded by barbed wire, but our stable was not guarded. When 100 or 150 allied airplanes flew over, the ground shook. When we heard the *Flieger-Alarm* sirens, we would jump into the surrounding fields and ditches, because it was so frightening. But the bombers flew further on to other cities. Each morning, older Germans arrived and took some of us for their everyday work.

In the mornings, we would come out from our sleeping places in *Lager Ostarbeiter*, already wearing our uniforms, and form a line of two abreast. The supervisors would be waiting for us. A few groups that had not been assigned to other supervisors were selected to fill the bomb crater holes. Our group would be no more than twenty or thirty people, and we would march under the supervisor's command, carrying our shovels on our shoulders. In our wooden clogs, we could be heard from afar. We sang our songs, and the Germans just looked at us.

Finally, we more or less completed our duties with the *Lager* in Wiesengrund, and the group was assigned to farmers. I worked for a farmer with a large farm, who already had one Pole, a Ukrainian woman, and a Frenchman working for him. This farmer had cows, horses, fowl, and forest-cutting work. My job was to clean up around the animals in the barn, but it did not please me. I stayed with that farmer for one week, and then I hauled my trunk on my back and walked out onto the road without letting anyone know. I headed toward the *Arbeitsamt*, the German employment office, in Mies, two or three miles away. The farmer, who was riding on a wagon with one of his workers, caught up with me and asked where I was going. He gave me a ride to the *Arbeitsamt*, and when we arrived, he spoke with the official there and left. I was left waiting in the office, wondering what would happen to me. Suddenly, a German came up to me, and I pulled out all of my documents—my Soviet passport, a photo of myself with my parents, and a document attesting to my having worked at the sewing factory named after Maxim Gorky in Demievtsi in Kyiv. I wanted to explain to the German that I was a factory worker and wanted to work in a factory. He slapped these documents out of my hand and did not even listen to what I had to say. I gathered my documents from the floor, and sat down wondering what would happen next. In about two hours, there came an older man, a German, who spoke with the man in the office. The older man was a farmer named Marschalek, and he took me to work on his farmstead. His family consisted of his wife, two sons, and a daughter and son-in-law who had twin daughters, both deaf and dumb. The sons and the son-in-law were called away for the war, so I worked in their stead until the end of the war in 1945.

L to R: 31. The Marschaleks. Unknown date and photographer. 32. A memorial card for their son, Franz, killed in the Second World War, front and back side.

Their farmstead was not large, maybe ten or twenty hectares—approximately fifty acres. When I was assigned to them, the entire farm was devoted to raising cattle. They owned five cows and two calves, and I plowed and seeded with the cows. All work was done with the cows. The Marschaleks had one other business, a *Gasthaus*—a tavern. They sold beer in bottles after the end of the workday in the evenings. Once a week, I would ride with the farmer to the brewery and bring back two barrels of beer from Mies, four or five kilometers away. We would always have the cows pull the wagon whenever it was required. Then we poured beer in smaller bottles, and in the evenings the neighboring Germans would come to buy their drinks. They would leave their empty bottles and go home with full ones. The beer was not made from barley, but it had the taste of beer.

My main job was outdoors and in the barn with the cattle, wherever the cows travelled, or in the fields. I also did other work, such as cutting grass for hay. Later, the farmer was given two Caucasian horses, so that the work became easier.

Gradually, I became familiar with this farm and the neighboring area. I found that on the neighboring farms there also worked two Ukrainian girls, a boy from Galicia, and a girl from the east. After work, we would get together to talk. We learned, who was from where, and so forth. My friends received a Ukrainian-language newspaper that was published in Berlin or Lviv, I can't now remember where. I borrowed it from them, and saw an advertisement in this newspaper that in the town of Prodebrady, Slovakia [now Czechia] (as far as I can recall) there was a Ukrainian Technical and Husbandry Institute, offering correspondence courses. There were several instructors. I chose to learn about the operation of and repair of all parts of an automobile engine. I wrote to the Institute that I wanted to study by correspondence, and some time later, I received a book titled *Automobile* in the mail. They also sent questions for each paragraph from beginning to end, and after I read the entire book, I wrote answers to all of the questions.

33. Wasyl Kushnir, July 24, 1944. Unknown photographer.

Correspondence I Received as a Forced Laborer in Germany

When I was in the custody of the Germans, I was able to communicate with my parents, friends, and relatives in other parts of Germany and in Ukraine through the German postal system. I purchased a two-part postcard, wrote my letter on the first card, and a return address on the second, attached card, glued stamps to go both ways, and the addressee could easily send me the second card back after writing the response. I was able to use this system during the period I worked in Wiesengrund and for the Marschaleks. I saved the return postcards, most of them written by my father to me during the first six months after I was taken to Germany.

Following is the documentary evidence of what was occurring in Ukraine under the German occupation. A few postcards are from my cousin, Ivan Pidkalyuk. He was the son of my mother Anna's brother Moisei. Ivan, who had also been conscripted by the Germans, was assigned to work in a coal mine in Saarland, an area on the border between Germany and France. These postcards, and their contents and associated information are reproduced here in the order in which I received them.

 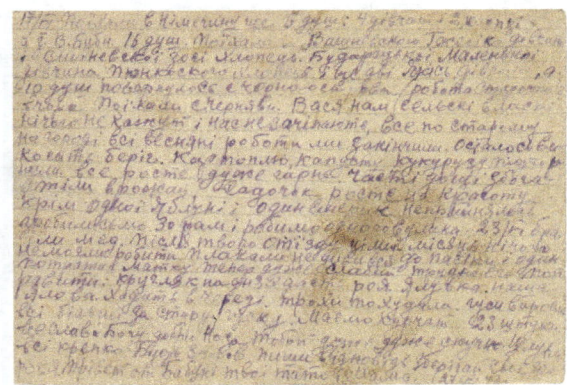

34. Postcard 1, dated June 27, 1943, front. 35. Postcard 1, dated June 27, 1943, back.

Postcard 1. June 27, 1943

To: Kuschnir Wasill, Ostarbeiter Lager, Wiesengrund, *Kreis* Mies.
From: Kuschnir Andrei, *Dorf* Nowa Bubnowka, *Kreis* Tscherno-Ostrowskii, *Gebiet* Kameniz Podolskii [later the *Gebiet* was reorganized. The new name was Proskurow].

Front of the card:
Good day, our son Vasya [Wasyl's parents always called him "Vasya," a short nickname for Wasyl]. We are all alive and well, and thus wish you all good fortune and health. Yesterday, on June 26, we received your first two postcards. Here at home, everything is as of old, everything is alright. It was difficult to wait for news from you for so long. A postcard from Kubich [a neighbor] arrived on June 19. Mother wrote you a postcard from his address. We don't know whether you received it. Glory be to God that you are well—that is to us a great joy. We wait for you very much, mother cries and is ill.

Back of the card:
On June 17, six more souls went to Germany: four girls and two boys, and from Velyka Bubnivka, sixteen souls went, [including] Vyshnevski's girl, Jessica and Zosia Vyshnevski's boy [both from Polish families], Little Budaretska's girl, Piunkovski's boy and two other girls [all Polish families], but ten souls returned from Chornyi Ostriv employment as monitors. Yesterday we travelled from Chernyava [the village where Wasyl's mother Anna was born]. Vasya, the village officials are not telling us anything and are not bothering us, all is unchanged. All springtime work is concluded in our garden. All that is left is to mow the shore [the edges of a former river, now a ravine, near their property]. We have raked over the potatoes, cabbage, and corn. Everything is growing very well. Frequent rains have increased the prospective harvest. The garden is growing beautifully, except for one apple tree and one pine tree which did not adjust well. We have made thirty frames [for the apiary] and are making one hive. On June 23 we took honey [from the hives]. After you left, we could not work for a whole month. We cried and did not look after the apiary, and one hive lost its queen and is now very weak. It is difficult to strengthen it. The *krukhliaka* [the round hive which produced new bees and where a new queen could be born] will produce a swarm in a day. Our large calf goes through the field grazing, but it has lost some weight. The geese have all grown larger than the old goose. We have twenty-three chicks. Everything is well, glory be to God, but we miss you very much. We all kiss you heartily, be well. Write your response, watch after your health.[1] Greetings from grandmother, your father, and mother. June 27, 1943.

---

1 Wasyl wrote his first postcards in May 1943. He had left his home on May 17, 1943.

Correspondence I Received as a Forced Laborer in Germany 43

 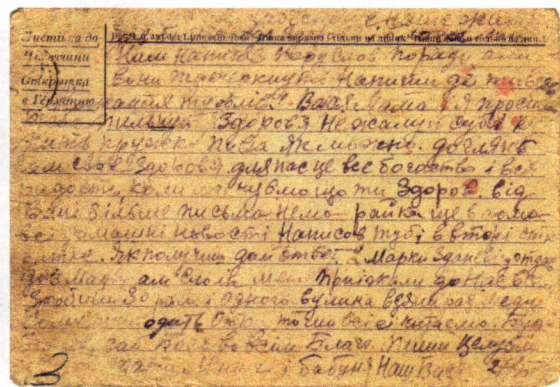

36. Postcard 2, dated June 27, 1943, front. 37. Postcard 2, dated June 27, 1943, back.

Postcard 2. June 27, 1943

Front of the card:
Good day, Vasya! We kiss you heartily, father, and mother, and grandmother. God give you health and good fortune and mercy and allow our quickly seeing you again. Today on Sunday I'm answering your two postcards. These are the first news from you. We received them yesterday, on June 26. Here at home, everything is as of old, everything is alright. Vasya, do not be dispirited, your work . . . [continued on the back]

Back of the card:
[. . . unintelligible] health; our life . . . [Unintelligible] had written several words of advice to us but they are crossed out. Please write, where did you get the leather shoes? Mother and I only ask you to watch your health, do not deny yourself a cup of beer if you can, watch over your health. Hearing that you are well is all our riches and happiness. From Vania [Ivan, the son of Moisei, the brother of Wasyl's mother Anna, who had been taken to the French border to work in a mine] there are no further letters. Raissa [Wasyl's cousin, the daughter of Anna's sister Maryna] is still at home. All news from home I described to you yesterday in the postcard. When you receive it, give an answer. I gave two stamps to Zdanevych, gave but a jar of honey [?]. They came to us in the village and built thirty frames [for honey] and one hive, they took once some honey. We had to give it up. [As for your] postcard, we all read it. Be well, may God bless everything. Write. We kiss you, father, mother, and grandmother, [we kiss] our Vasya. June 27, 1943.

44 | Epic Journey

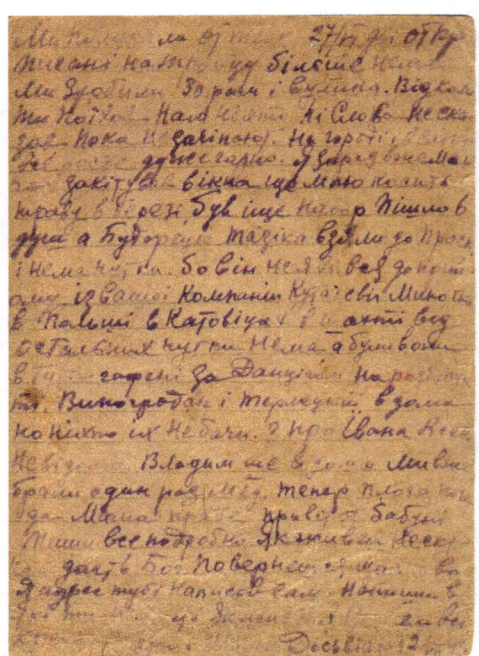

38. Postcard 3, dated July 2, 1943, front. 39. Postcard 3, dated July 2, 1943, back.

Postcard 3. July 2, 1943

Front of the card:
Good day, Vasya! Greetings from father and mother. This is the fourth postcard we are writing. We don't know whether you have received them all. We are all alive and well. Everything here is alright. We have cultivated the garden. Mother and I plead that you watch over your health, do not deny yourself any foods, do not be stingy with yourself.

Back of the card:
We received from you, on June 27, two postcards written [unintelligible]. There are no others. We built thirty frames and a hive. From the time you left, no one has said a word to us; thus far, no one is touching us. In our market-garden and orchard, all is growing very nicely. I now have time to caulk the windows, and still have to mow the grass on the shore. There was another call-up. [The Germans recruited more people to work in Germany.] Six souls went, and Thaddeus Budaretski was taken to Proskuriv, and no word is heard, because he has not been seen before the call-up. [It could be that partisans, Ukrainian or Communist, took him, or he was executed.] From your company [of friends], Mykola Kutasevych is in Poland, in Katowice. [He works there] in a coal mine, and we have

no more reports [from him]. And others were in the work camp beyond Danzig [now Gdan'sk]. On the [unintelligible], Vynohradski and Terletski are at home, but no one has seen them. About Ksenia's Ivan, we know nothing. Vladim [the son of Wasyl's aunt Domakha] is still at home. We have already taken honey once. It is a bad time now. Mother forwards greetings from granny. Write everything about you, [write] how you are doing, do not pine. God grant that you will return safely. I wrote your address myself. Write about your news, how you are living? Hearty kisses from all, father, mother. Goodbye. July 2, 1943.

 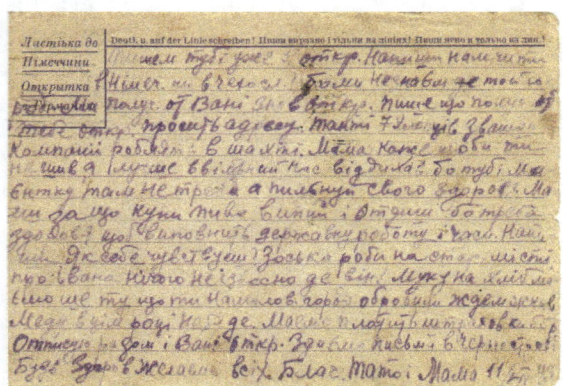

40. Postcard 4, dated July 11, 1943, front. 41. Postcard 4, dated July 11, 1943, back.

Postcard 4. July 11, 1943

Front of the card:
Good day, Vasya! Greetings from us all, we wish you all mercies of our Father Jesus Christ! We received your third postcard. Thank God that you are well. We are also all alive and well and everything here is all right, thank God. Within the household it is thus: we have mown and gathered the hay, we have a new family of bees, we are taking no more honey because there is no more. The weather is very bad. No one is forcing us to work [in the commune].

Back of the card.
We have already written five postcards. Write to us whether you are in Germany or Czechoslovakia, because we don't know where. [Unintelligible.] We received another postcard from Vanya [Ivan Pidkalyuk]. He says that he received a postcard from you and asks for your address. The seven boys from your company are working in a coal mine. Mother says that you should not sew but better rest in your free time, because you do not need possessions there. Better watch over your health. If you have something that would allow you to buy a beer, drink it and relax, because you need your health to carry out the country's work [rebuilding German infrastructure after the bombing by the Allies], and to find the time. How do you feel? Zoska is working at her old job [Wasyl's father did not want

to specify that she was a translator]. About Ivan nothing is known; where is he? We have the flour for bread that you had ground.² We have fenced the garden and await the harvest. There will be no honey this year. We will have to pay a tax of fifty-five rubles. I will also write a reply to Vania's postcard. We mail the letters in Chornyi Ostriv [a trade town with a large Jewish population]. Be well, we wish you all blessings, father and mother. July 11, 1943.

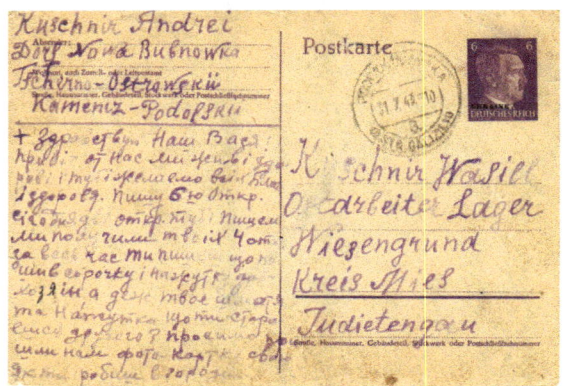 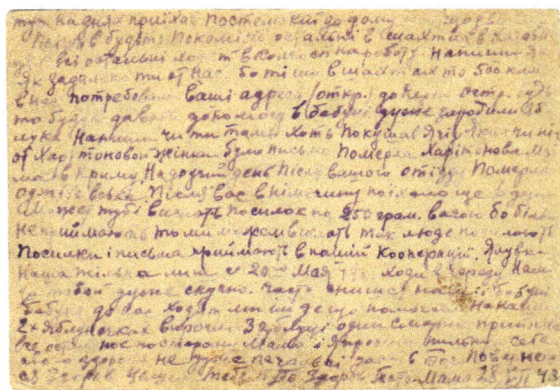

42. Postcard 5, dated July 28, 1943, front. 43. Postcard 5, dated July 28, 1943, back.

Postcard 5. July 28, 1943

Front of the card:
Good day, our Vasya! Greetings from us all. We are alive and well, and wish you all of God's blessings and health. I am writing the sixth postcard. We received your four postcards and all the time you write that you sewed a shirt, and a jacket was given to you by the landlord, but where are your clothes and jacket if you need new ones? We ask that you send us a photo showing you how you work in the city.

Back of the card.
Several days ago, Postelski arrived home. Where [illegible] he ostensibly rode to the Commission [which sent people to Germany] to work in the mines in Katowice. The others are going to work in the commune. Write about how far you are from us. Because those in the mines are 500 km [away]. We need your address [for cards] to Chornyi Ostriv so that we can give you assistance. At your grandmother's, we have a great apple harvest. Write whether you have at least tasted some cherries or not. We received a letter from Kharitonov's wife. Kharitonov's mother died in Crimea the second day after you left [when Wasyl and the others were taken from the village]. Ms. Odzhekhovska

---

2   Before he was taken by the Germans, Wasyl had ground the grain with a wooden box called *zharna*. The grain was placed on the top of this box and fell into an opening. When the stone wheel turned over a bottom wheel, the grain was ground, and flour came out of a hole on the bottom.

died. After you, six other souls went to Germany. Is it possible to send you a package of 250 grams? The others would not accept it. But we can send, as people send packages and letters that are accepted in our store. Our calf Yaluvka is pregnant from May 20, 1943, she has been going with the shepherd to the pasture. We are very lonely without you. We and grandmother often dream [about you]. Grandmother walks over to us and helps a little. On our two apple trees, three types of apples have grown. One *smerek* [a type of pine tree] has taken root. Everything else is as of old. Mother and I beg you to watch your health. Don't worry. God grant you will return healthy. Kissing you, be well, father, mother. July 28, 1943.

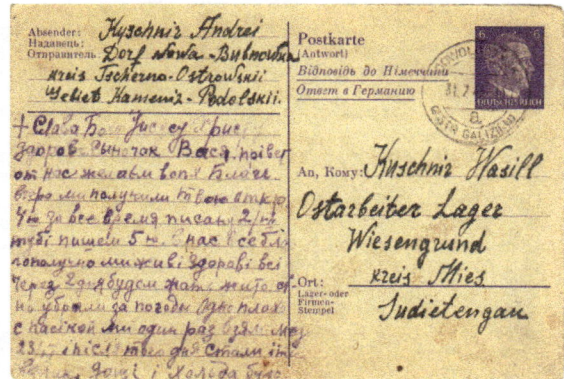 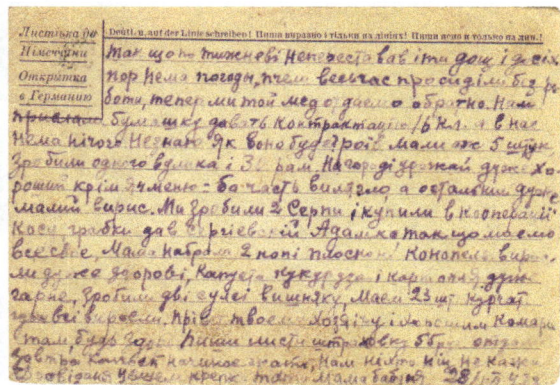

44. Postcard 6, dated July 28, 1943, front. 45. Postcard 6, dated July 28, 1943, back.

Postcard 6. July 28, 1943

Front of the card:
Glory to the Lord Jesus Christ. Greetings, dear son Vasya. Greetings from us, we wish you all blessings. Yesterday we received your postcard, the fourth for the entire period, written on July 7. We are writing our fifth postcard to you. Here, everything is well, we are all well and healthy. In two days we will harvest rye. We have gathered the hay during good weather. The only problem is with the beehives. We took honey only once, on June 23. After that, great rains fell, and it has been cold.

Back of the card:
After a week the rain didn't stop and until now we have not had good weather. The bees have spent the whole time without work. Now we are giving that honey back [to the bees, so that they might live]. They sent us a piece of paper [requesting] to give away sixteen kilograms. But we have nothing. I don't know what will happen. We had five new families of bees, we made one hive and thirty frames. In our kitchen garden, the harvest is very good except barley—because a portion was laid down and the last portion grew very small. We made two sickles and

bought a scythe from the store; a rake was provided by Serhievski's Adamko, so that we have everything of our own. Mother gathered two *kipas* [one *kipa* equals sixteen sheaves] of *ploskony* [hemp without seeds]. The [usual] hemp grew very healthy, the cabbage, corn, and potatoes were very good; we made two *sulii* [six liters] of cherry syrup. We have twenty-three chickens, they have all grown. We greet your landlord and your good commander [apparently, Marschalek, the farmer to which Wasyl was assigned]. Be well, write letters. We have paid the tax of fifty-five rubles. Tomorrow we begin to reap the rye, no one says anything about it to us. So long, we kiss you heartily, father, mother, and grandmother. July 28, 1943.

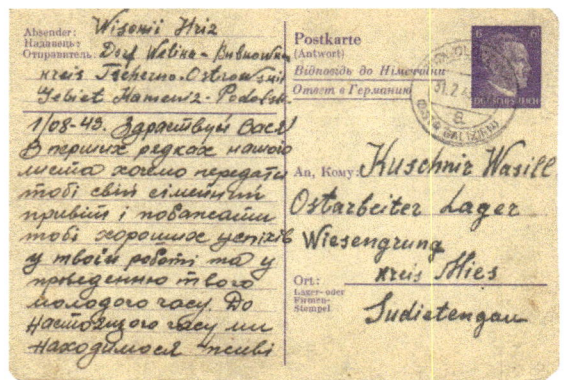 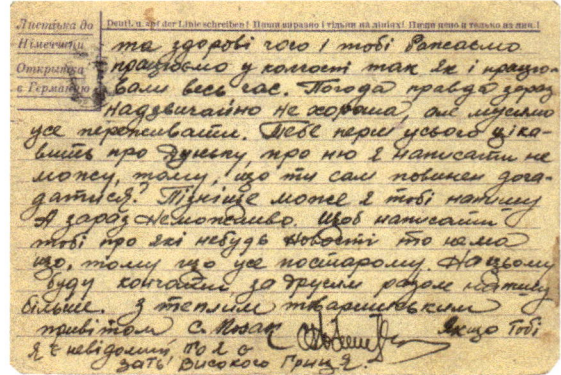

46. Postcard 7, dated August 1, 1943, front. 47. Postcard 7, dated August 1, 1943, back.

Postcard 7. August 1, 1943

Front of the card:
Good day, Vasya
In the first lines of our letter, we want to send you our family greeting and wish you good success in your work as your youthful time carries forth. As of now, we find ourselves alive . . .

Back of the card:
. . . and well, which is what we wish for you. We are working at the commune, just as we have worked the whole time. To say the truth, the weather at this time is exceptionally not good, but we must suffer it. You are first of all interested in Dunka's fate, but about her I cannot write. Why? You should have already guessed it yourself. Later, maybe, I will write to you about it, but now it is not possible. [Dunka, daughter of Vysokyi Hrytz, was a close young female acquaintance, maybe a girlfriend, of Wasyl's.] It is useless to write to you about any kind of news, because everything is as of old. On this, I will end. Next time I will write more. With warm friendly greetings, C. Nosak. In

case you are not familiar with me, I am the son-in-law of Vysokyi Hrytz. [Vysokyi Hrytz, or "Tall Greg(ory)," was with Wasyl's father Andrei in Petliura's army and also served time with him in Siberia.]

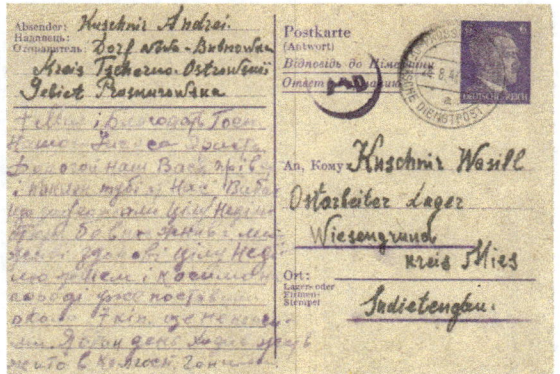

48. Postcard 8, dated August 7, 1943, front. 49. Postcard 8, dated August 7, 1943, back.

Postcard 8. August 7, 1943

Front of the card:
Peace and blessings of our Lord Jesus Christ. Our dear Vasya, greetings and a bow to you from us. Forgive that we waited a whole week to [write a] postcard because we have been harvesting. We are alive and well. All week we have been reaping and scything in our field. We have already set forth about seven *kipas*. We have not finished yet. One day I went to reap rye in the commune. They forced me.

Back of the card:
July 7, 1943
Vysoka [probably meaning Vysokyi Hrytz's wife] came to us. We gave her your postcard and received two postcards. Dun'ka sits at home and does not show herself. Vasya, everyone here is very amazed at your postcards because you so well write boasting about your job and life. Your postcards cheer us very much, [as we know] that all is well with you, glory be to God. Even the head of the village is amazed at this. We received your six postcards—we write to you our seventh. Domka's [son] Vladimka is getting ready for Germany. Vasya, here your postcards are read by the village council, everyone is very interested. About our housekeeping we have already written to you. There is no specific news. Write more often because Kutovych [a young man from a neighbor's family, who used to live in the fourth house from the Kushnirs] writes much more and often. Greetings to your landlord and his wife. Be well. God grant it that you return soon to us. Father. Mother, 7/VIII.

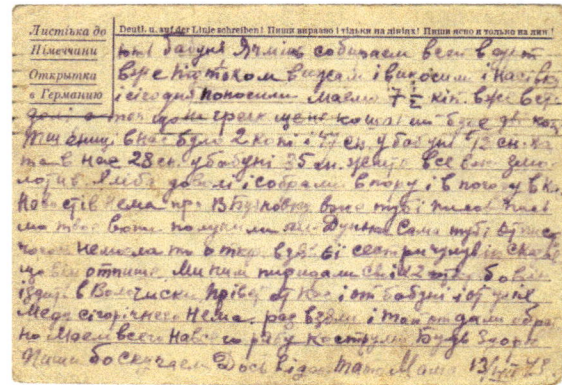

50. Postcard 9, dated August 13, 1943, front. 51. Postcard 9, dated August 13, 1943, back.

Postcard 9. August 13, 1943

Front of the card:
Greetings, Vasya, we wish you all good blessings. Vasya, we are all well. We received all of your postcards. Thank you for writing. On August 10 we received a postcard, and we also received two more, on July 18 and 25. We are responding to all your postcards. Today, on August 13, we send several packages. Mother will write because I don't know whether they will all be accepted. So far we have prepared nine items. Here we are harvesting, we are ourselves gathering bread, it is ground for us by . . .

Back of the card:
. . . grandmother. As for barley, we are reaping it all together, the entire field has been reaped and the grain has been carried out and we now have seven and a half *kipas* in the barn. And then there is buckwheat, which we are not harvesting yet—there will be two more *kipas*. At grandmother's there are twelve sheaves, and we have twenty-eight sheaves. Grandmother has thirty-five sheaves of wheat. All of that has been ground. There is enough bread, and we have collected it in good weather. [Unintelligible.] There is no news. I have already written you a letter about Velyka Bubnivka. We have received your letter, Dun'ka will write to you herself, for some reason she couldn't. Her sister's husband took them and said he would write. We gave him our two postcards because he goes to Volochysk [a town on the border of Ukraine and Poland]. Greetings from us and from grandmother, and from everyone. Honey from this year there is none. We took it once, and gave it away [back to the bees] immediately. We only have that in the speckled pot. Be well and write because we miss you. Goodbye, father and mother. August 13, 1943.

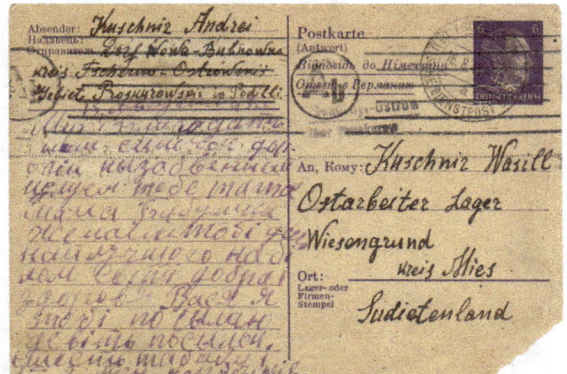 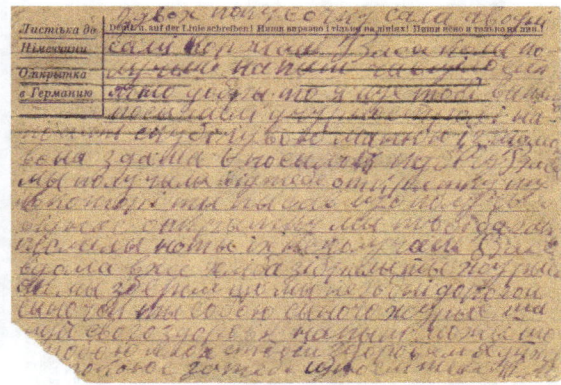

52. Postcard 10, dated August 13, 1943, front. 53. Postcard 10, dated August 13, 1943, back.

Postcard 10. August 13, 1943

Front of the card:
Peace and blessings, [unintelligible] dear unforgotten son. We kiss you, your father, mother, and grandmother. We wish you all the best in the whole world, fortune and health. Vasya, I am sending you nine packages, there are six of tobacco and three measures of cookies. [Wasyl had written his parents that he could exchange tobacco for bread with Czechs in Germany.]

Back of the card:
Vasya, when you receive them, write whether the baked goods have arrived safely. If all is well, then I will send you more. We are sending by way of Chornyi Ostriv. It [the package] is in the mail. Mother [?] delivered six packages of tobacco. Vasya, we received a postcard from you, the one in which you wrote that you received a postcard from us. We wrote to you very often, but you are not receiving them.[3] Vasya, at home we have already gathered the bread grain. You are worried how we harvested, that we are hungry. Dear son, you better worry about yourself and watch your health. Write how your health is. I am very worried about you. Kissing you, Mama.

---

3   Apparently, while mail through the German postcard system was delivered (albeit with censorship), the mail sent by Wasyl's parents through any other postal system that may have existed did not reach the addressees.

 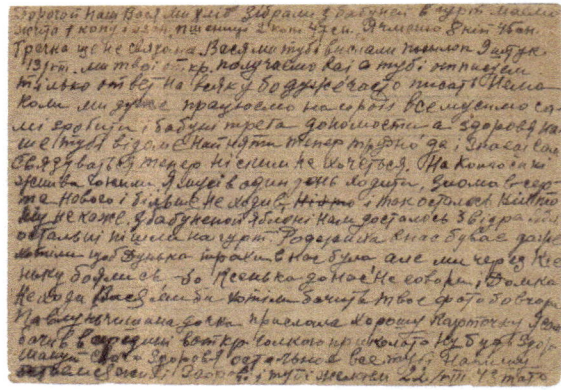

54. Postcard 11, dated August 22, 1943, front. 55. Postcard 11, dated August 22, 1943, back.

Postcard 11. August 22, 1943

Front of the card:
Glory to the Lord Jesus Christ. Vasya, this is to let you know that we are all alive and well. We wish you the same, sending you all blessings and good health. Son, here with us everything is well, we are already finishing the harvest. What is left is to tie up the buckwheat, and plow up for the winter, but they are not giving us horses. We are forced, with mother, to dig with a shovel. Already we have dug up a piece by the house on our half of the part that is left after reaping, with rough stalks sticking out.

Back of the card:
Our dear Vasya, we have harvested the bread [wheat and rye], ours and grandmother's together. We have one *kipa* of rye and twelve extra sheaves; of wheat we have two *kipas* and forty-seven sheaves. Of barley, eight *kipas*, and forty-five sheaves. The buckwheat is not yet tied up. Vasya, we have sent to you nine packages on August 13. We received all of your postcards, and are responding to them. We are answering as best we can, because there is not enough time for us to write often. We are working hard in the field because we have to do everything ourselves and must help grandmother. And our health is known to you [Andrei's leg rendered him partially an invalid]. It is now difficult to hire someone, and you know yourself that it is not desirable to tie oneself to anyone. People were driven to work on the commune. I had to go one day, broke the new sickle, and afterwards did not go. And thus they left it, no one said anything. From grandmother's apple tree we got three pails of apples [Fuji apples—very large, succulent. This tree had never borne apples. Wasyl's grandfather Semen had planted it, and his grandmother had driven a tine from a rake into the root.]. The rest [of the apples] went to the [commune] herd. Rodorykha [a neighbor?] stops with us, we have wanted for Dun′ka [possibly here Andrei means Domka, a form of Domakha, the name of his sister] to be with us, but we were afraid because of Ksenia [Ksenia is Andrei's

other sister], because Ksenia talks to us and Domka does not visit. Vasya, we would like to see your photo because yesterday Pavlunchykhyn's daughter sent us a beautiful card. I saw the card myself, pinned by a needle through its center. Well, be well, watch your heath; I will write to you about the rest. We remain well, and wish you the same. July 22, 1943. Father.

 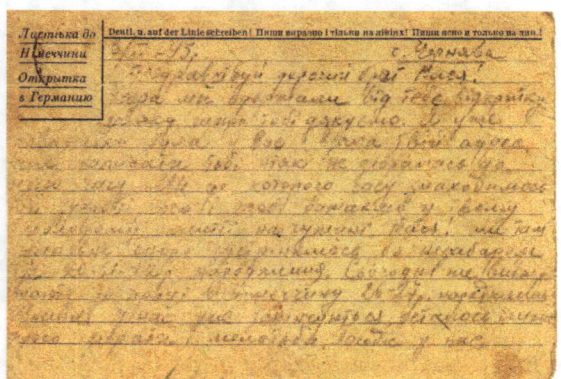

56. Postcard 12, dated September 3, 1943, front. 57. Postcard 12, dated September 3, 1943, back.

Postcard 12. September 3, 1943

From: *selo* Chernaya, Hibrak Raissa K. [Karpivna—patronymic, from the name of her father, Karpo. Raissa's mother Maryna was one of Anna Kushnir's sisters.]

Front of the card:
. . . Right now the rains are coming through, but they are needed. They will be planting the winter rye. Vasya, write more often and I will answer you and will give more details about everything. In the meantime, stay well. Thank you for remembering, and my respects to you. Sister [actually, Wasyl's cousin] Raissa. Please write.

Back of the card:
Greetings, dear brother Vasya! Yesterday, we received your postcard, for which we heartily thank you. It has been a long time since I was at your family's. I obtained your address so that I could write to you. I haven't been able to do that until this time. At this time we find ourselves well, and we wish you [well] in your current life in a foreign land. Vasya! We will certainly meet soon there because they are taking everyone from twenty or twenty-two years of age. Today, twenty-six- and twenty-seven-year-olds are leaving for work in Germany. Harvesting is close to completion here, all that is left is millet, it has been gathered and the milling has begun.

L to R: 58. Wasyl's uncle Ivan yuk (his mother Anna's brother), cousin Raissa, and Raissa's husband Andrei Yaremchuk, February 12, 1945. Unknown photographer. 59. Raissa Yaremchuk, her second husband (name unknown), and daughters Marina, Lena, and Lyudmila, 1991. Unknown photographer. Raissa died around 2010.

60. Postcard 13, dated September 4, 1943, front. 61. Postcard 13, dated September 4, 1943, back.

Postcard 13. September 4, 1943

Front of the card:
Glory to Lord Jesus Christ. Our esteemed and dear son Vasya. Greetings from us, wishing you all blessings and good health. We are sending you today one package of tobacco in weight of one *kilo* [about 2 lbs], and we inform

you that we are all alive, well, and that all here is good. We finished reaping and dug up the stalks left after that. Thanks God. F. Bukhanovski came to Velyka Bubnivka from Poltava.

Back of the card:
... with two great horses, we hired him and he plowed the kitchen garden, [tearing] all of the left-over stalks wherever they were. We planted wheat on both halves—about seven *puds* [1 *kilo* is 2 lbs, and 16 *kilos* make 1 *pud*; therefore 7 *puds* are about 224 lbs]. The commune allowed us to borrow a plow, a rake, and a *borin* [another farming instrument], and after two full days, we did all this. This cost us 5 *puds* of barley grain and one *pud* of winter wheat/rye mixture. [This mixture is planted in autumn, develops under snow, and is reaped at the end of summer.] Now, we have only to dig up six *puds* of potatoes, take down the corn, and plant the rye. We planted the wheat during the beautiful weather of August 31, and on September 7, according to the new calendar, it is starting to come up. Dear Vasya, mother and I beg that you watch after your health, do not be stingy about your well-being and do not save your money. Do not buy a watch or anything else buy, only food, so that you can stay well. Health is a greater gift from God. When we hear that you are healthy, it is a great joy for us. Here, thirteen boys and girls are leaving for Germany on the sixth or the ninth of the month. With this, be well, we kiss you heartily. Father and Mother. We await your reply. We received a card from Wiesengrund with another postcard. Goodbye. September 4, 1943.

 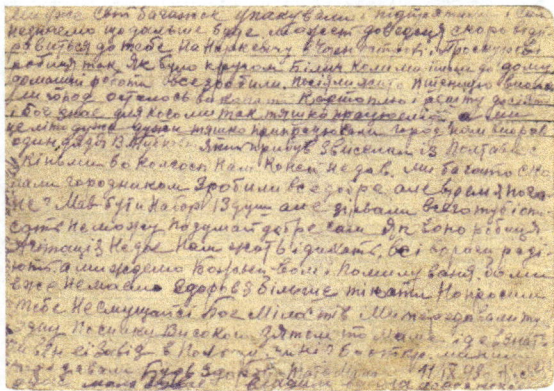

62. Postcard 14, dated September 11, 1943, front. 63. Postcard 14, dated September 11, 1943, back.

Postcard 14. September 11, 1943

Front of the card:
Glory to the Lord Jesus Christ. Greetings, our Vasya. Greetings from us and wishes for good health and all blessings. We are all, so far, alive and well, and so far all is well. I have written to you about this misfortune and do not know what to do. Our situation right now is as it was in Bilychi in the previous days of our lives. And the work is

not going well. Vasya, we received the postcard you wrote on August 6th. In it you wrote that you have experienced a strain and are sitting on [unintelligible] . . .

Back of the card:
We have already brought in all of our belongings and fixed things up, and do not know what will happen next. Maybe it will turn out so that we must direct ourselves to you by way of Narkevich. In Chornyi Ostriv and Proskuriv there are occurrences such as happened around Bilychi when we were walking home [when Wasyl and his father were traveling back from Bilychi to Nova Bubnivka]. All of the work around the house was completed. We planted the wheat and the rye, the kitchen garden has been put to order. We now only have to dig up the potatoes and finish planting, and God knows for whom. We are working so hard, we have worked very hard all summer. Our garden was plowed by a fellow from Velyka Bubnivka who was sent from Poltava [people from Poltava were arriving, escaping from the Bolsheviks] with horses, because the commune would not give us horses. We plowed much with the shovel and did everything well. But maybe the timing was bad? They were to be taking people to Germany [for forced labor], they took but thirteen souls, but I cannot write about everything, you must think about it yourself. The propaganda [political propaganda by the Communists] does not let us live and breathe. [Apparently, the war was going badly for the Germans.] All enemies are gleeful, and we are awaiting God's will and mercy because we no longer have the health to escape. But we ask you to not be saddened by God's mercies. We gave one package to Vysokyi's son in law, so mother is going to find out where he took it, to the post office or not. We also left a postcard [with him], but we do not know whether he took it to Poland or not. Because the postcard we [unintelligible] handed over. Be well, father, mother. September 11, 1943. Until we see each other again. Very little [unintelligible].

 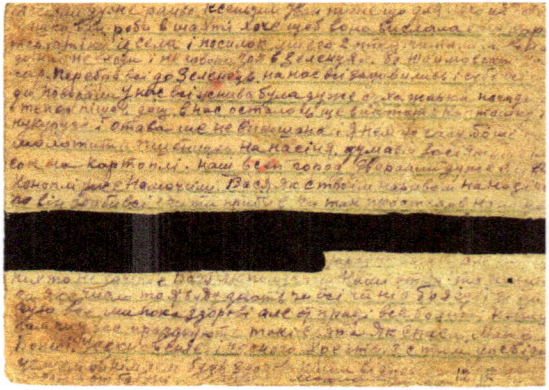

64. Postcard 15, dated September 12, 1943, front. 65. Postcard 15, dated September 12, 1943, back.

Postcard 15. September 12, 1943

Front of the card:
Glory to the Lord Jesus Christ. Vasya, greetings and a bow to you. We wish you all blessings. With us, everything is well so far. I'm writing to you today about this postcard and about everything [that happens to us]. Today we are sending the sixteenth postcard. You write that so far, you have received six. The last ones are still on the way. Our grandmother is going to the harvest for the stalks. She gathered a whole [abandoned] beehive [routinely used to collect grain]. Vasya, we wish you could see our beautiful winter wheat in our kitchen garden, as it is very green. Wheat and rye are coming up.

Back of the card:
Winter has come very early. Ksenia's Ivan [Ksenia was Andrei's sister; Ivan Mashtaler was her husband, taken for slave labor by the Germans] writes that for him [Ivan] his work is very hard. He works in the mine. [Interestingly, Ivan Moiseievych Pidkalyuk, Anna Kushnir's nephew, son of her brother Moisei, was also forced to work in a mine.] She asks that we send them special food from the *selo* and packages. We read his two postcards. She does not talk to her Zoia from Zelenya [unintelligible]. Everyone has been watching us and everything has been plowed. Here, the period of reaping was very hot and dry, but now the rains have come. We have yet to dig up the potatoes and gather the corn, and the grass needs mowing, and I don't have the time because the wheat has not been ground into flour. We are thinking to plant a piece of land with potatoes. Our entire kitchen garden has been wonderfully plowed. The hemp has been soaked [hemp was planted into water, and women had to get into the water to pull it out—many got sick and even died.] Vasya, how is the growth on your leg, what happened to it? Did you hurt it, did you catch cold? [Censored.] Right now, there is no [unintelligible]. No one is bothering us. Vasya, when you receive our postcards, let us know the date, and I will know if they are all coming through or not. I feel worse. All of us are currently healthy, but everything hurts from working. Do they celebrate holidays such as Spasy [a sequence of holidays when people take fruits and vegetable to church for blessing], Mother of God, Beheading of John the Baptist, and the True Christ there? With this, goodbye, we send you kisses and hugs and wish you well. Write a reply. Greetings from grandmother. Father and Mother, November 12, 1943.

 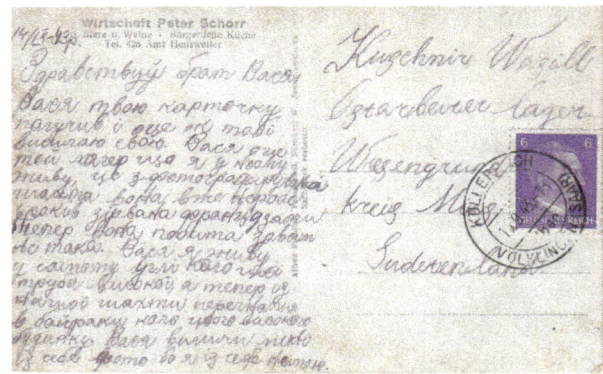

66. Postcard 16, dated September 11, 1943, front. 67. Postcard 16, dated September 11, 1943, back.

Postcard 16. September 11, 1943

This card was written by Ivan Moiseievych Pidkalyuk, Wasyl's cousin from his mother's side. He was taken to forced labor in Dilsburg/Saar coal mine pictured on the front of the card.

Greetings, brother Vasya
I received your postcard and here I am writing you mine. This is the barracks where I live. This is a photograph of the mine—it has been closed for six years, after it was blown up by the French. Now it is closed with wooden planks and not at all as pictured. Vasya, I live in the far corner near the tall pipe, and now from our mine they transferred everyone to barracks by the tall building. Vasya, send me a photo of yourself, because I don't have any photos of myself.

 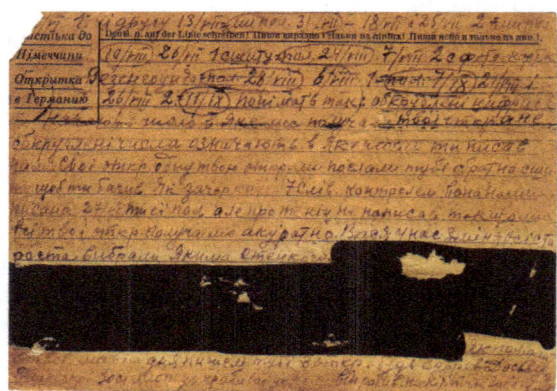

68. Postcard 17, dated September 12, 1943, front. 69. Postcard 17, September 12, 1943, back.

Postcard 17. September 12, 1943

Front of the card:

Glory to the Lord Jesus Christ. Good day, Vasya. We are alive and well and wish you all blessings. Yesterday evening we received your two postcards written 21/VIII and 26 [August 21 and 26]. Thank God that you are well and making us happy with your life. [Unintelligible] write more and so we will [unintelligible] for all [unintelligible] and all fourteen postcards written on 9/VI. We received two postcards on 26/VI; the postcard from 23/VI we received on 10/VII, and the postcard from 1/VII we received on 27/VII. Vasya, write what you discuss with your gathered companions.

Back of the card:

. . . VI we had one, and your second postcard from 13/VII we received on 31/VII, then we received your two postcards from 18/VII and 25/VII on 10/VIII. One sewn postcard from 26/VII we received on 24/VIII, and on 28/VIII we received a two-page photo card of Wiesengrund, sent on 7/VIII. The postcard from 6/VIII was received on 7/IX, and the two postcards from 21/VIII and 26/VIII were received on 11/IX. The understanding is thus the circled numbers indicate the date we received your postcards and the uncircled ones indicate the date you wrote to us. One of your cards we sent back to you so that you could see how seven words were blacked out [censored]. It was written on 27/VI, you received it but didn't write to us about this. So we are receiving your postcards accurately. Vasya, here we have is a new village head, they elected Yukim Stetsko [censored—blacked out]. When you receive a response [unintelligible] day we write you 3 postcards. Be well, so long. Write. Zosya Vyshnevski's son came home. He worked [in Germany] at a brick factory.

 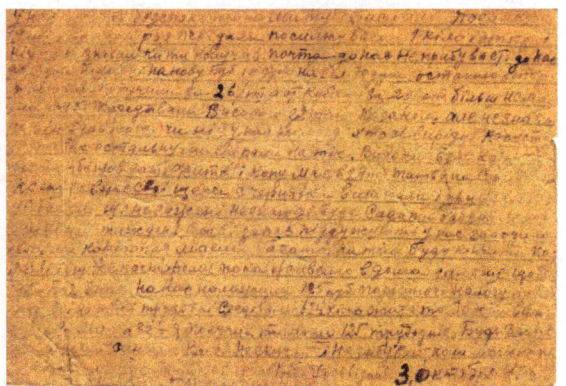

70. Postcard 18, dated October 3, 1943, front. 71. Postcard 18, dated October 3, 1943, back.

Postcard 18. October 3, 1943

Front of the card:
Glory to the Lord Jesus Christ. Good health, our dear son Vasya. Greetings from us, we wish you all blessings. Vasya, we are all well, still in place, and at home everything is satisfactory. In our kitchen garden we finished all work and planted rye and wheat by the entrance near the buckwheat and also on Grandmother's half. We have not received postcards from you for three weeks.

Back of the card:
Here [unintelligible] without peace [unintelligible]. We sent you nine packages and handed over one package weighing 1 kilo and a postcard. We don't know whether you received any of this. Mail does not come to us [unintelligible] to Nova Bubnivka. Ten souls on [unintelligible] . . . seventy souls. We received your latest postcard on 26/VIII and a postcard from Kubich [a neighbor] 29/VIII, but no more. We sent [a message] by way of Vysokyi's *kozak* [the term, in this context, could mean a "young buck" or a military man] son-in-law, but we don't know whether he delivered it or not. In our garden, someone cut out the cabbage [unintelligible], the last one they took from outside the yard. Vysokyi took [unintelligible]. Ksenia already took her pinched seedlings from [village] Chernyava, dug them up and brought to grandmother. They are still unplanted, and I don't know where granny will plant them. [Unintelligible] at the end of the week are getting better. We had a wonderful potato harvest, and gathered much. On this I will conclude [unintelligible]. All is as of old, and so far, we are living in our house. What will happen in the future, God knows. They placed a tax of 125 rubles on each soul, they had tracked your work days here. . . . I receive [unintelligible] 62½ kilograms rye, and [unintelligible] 64 [unintelligible], and 32 ½. You have 125 work days. Be well, Vasya, don't be sad and don't forget, when you can [unintelligible]. So long. October 3, 43.

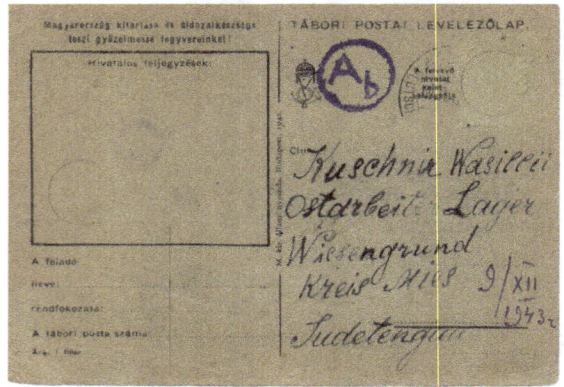 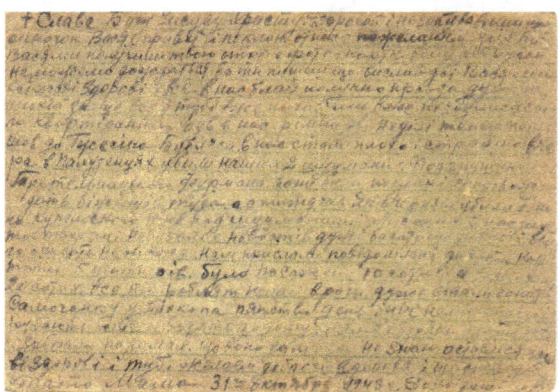

72. Postcard 19, dated October 31, 1943, front. 73. Postcard 19, dated October 31, 1943, back.

Correspondence I Received as a Forced Laborer in Germany | 61

Postcard 19. October 31, 1943

Back of the card:

Glory to the Lord Jesus Christ. Dear and unforgotten son of ours, Vasya. Greetings and a bow from us, and we wish you all blessings. Vasya, we received your postcard and photo, as well as your card. Both [unintelligible] . . . we cannot wait, because you write that you sent two. Vasya, we are all alive, well, and all is well. Truth be told, it is very uncertain here, as I have already written. We have already gotten rid of [unintelligible] tenant, he was here only two weeks, now he has gone to Jessika Bublias. Here it has become bad and frightening, yesterday in Pakhutyntsi [a neighboring village] they killed two *Schutzmänner*,[4] Podhurshyn and Tremelnytskyi, and a *Fuhrmann*.[5] They were sent to direct refugees there. And a week ago, when in Chernyava . . . there was killed in Kupelskyi [a town, very Jewish] . . . a *Schutzmann* [unintelligible]. . . . Here on our friends there haven't been any. There is a lot of news but I cannot write all of them. We received an announcement that we must give 5 *tsentnars* [1 *tsentnar* = 100 kilograms] of potatoes. We had planted ten hundred [unintelligible] . . . twenty hundred. . . . all this is done by our enemies. In [village] Prokop they have started making a lot of moonshine. Drunkenness day and night, one cannot . . . [unintelligible] and carry/drive home. And bread and beets are beginning, they are taking them from the houses. What will happen now, I don't know. We remain all healthy, and we wish you good health and fortune. Father, Mother, 31 October, 1943. Goodbye.

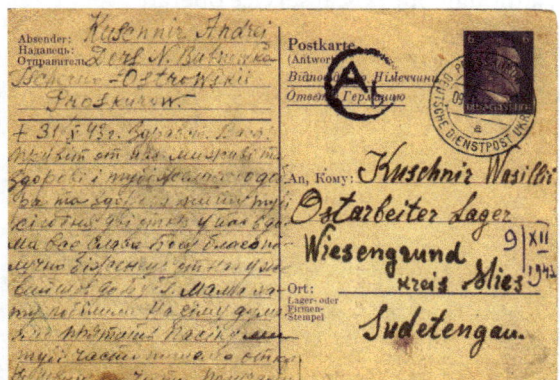

74. Postcard 20, dated October 31, 1943, front. 75. Postcard 20, dated October 31, 1943, back.

---

4 As noted earlier, in the village of Pakhutyntsi in 1932, fifty houses were left empty due to the starvation genocide, the Holodomor, brought by Stalin upon the Ukrainian people, and beggars went from house to house. When the Germans occupied the region, they created a militia called *Schutzmänner* (singular: *Schutzmann*).

5 German: coach driver.

Postcard 20. October 31, 1943

Front of the card:
31/X, 43. Greetings, Vasya! Best regards from us, we are alive and well and wish good fortune and health to you. I am writing two postcards to you today. Here at home everything is all right, glory be to God. The *bizhenets* [runaway from Poltava] has already gone away to Bubnivka. Mother has painted the inside of the house readying it for winter. We now plan to put the apiary in order. We want to write postcards to you more often, but we don't know whether you receive them.

Back of the card:
Our news is as follows: yesterday evening they [the Communist partisans] killed Podhrushyn and the *Fuhrmann*, our *Schutzmänner* in Pakhutyntsi. On October 22 we received your photo card sent on October 6, but the second card has not come. Our young cow will have a calf. We have six geese and twenty-one chickens. We also have a new sack of wheat and we traded rye for cabbage. We have everything to beyond limits. But God knows who will use it all because the times are very difficult. Justin gave us a whole can of kerosene. They ground flour for us and we received almost a whole sack of small grain. I ground the bread [grain], and got eight *kipas* of barley and two *kipas* of buckwheat. Of grain [oats, wheat, etc.] we have in our field 38 *soty* [one hectare contains 100 *soty*] on our half. It is very large and green and in places it lays down. Please write, although our postal service operates very weakly. Be well, our dear son, we kiss you heartily. Father and Mother, October 31, 1943. Goodbye.

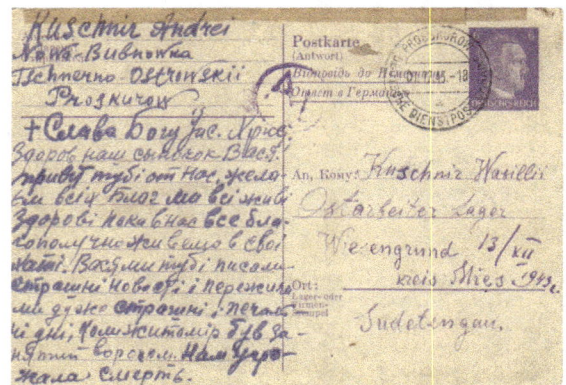 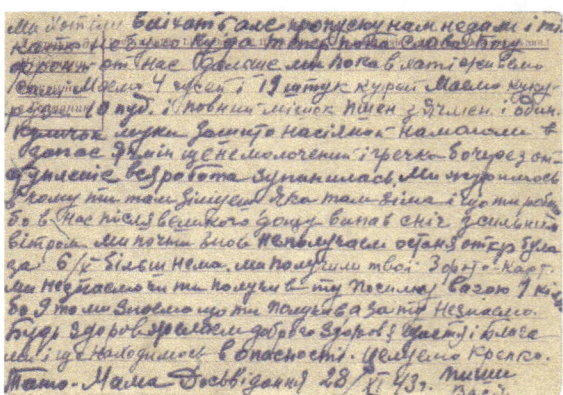

76. Postcard 21, dated November 28, 1943, front. 77. Postcard 21, dated November 28, 1943, back.

Postcard 21. November 28, 1943

Front of the card:
Glory to the Lord Jesus Christ. Good health to you, our dear son Vasya. We send our greetings and wish for all blessings. We are all alive, healthy, and so far, all is well, we are living in our own house. Vasya, we wrote to you about the terrible news, and have survived very frightful and dangerous days when Zhytomyr [a city 200 kilometers from Nova Bubnivka] was taken over by the enemy. We were threatened with death.

Back of the card:
We wanted to escape, but they would not give us a pass, and there was nowhere to escape to. For now, glory be to God, the front is further from us. We now live in our house by ourselves. We have four geese and nineteen chickens. We also have ten *puds* of corn and a whole bag of wheat and barley, as well as one small sewn up bag of seeds, not ground, in reserve. The barley is not ground, and neither is the buckwheat. Because of the [German] withdrawal, all work has stopped. We are worried thinking which winter clothes you have, what the winter there is like, and what you are doing. Here, after a big rain, snow fell and there is a strong wind. We do not receive any mail at all. Your last postcard was from 6/X, and there are no more. We received your three photo cards, but we don't know if you received the package weighing one kilo—we know you received nine packages, but of that one we don't know. Stay healthy, we wish you good heath, fortune, and blessings. We still find ourselves in danger. We kiss you heartily, Father, Mother. Goodbye. 28/XI, 1943. Write, Vasya.

 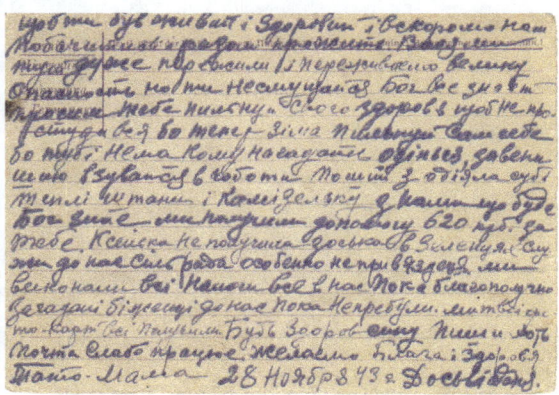

78. Postcard 22, dated November 28, 1943, front. 79. Postcard 22, dated November 28, 1943, back.

64 | Epic Journey

Postcard 22. November 28, 1943

Front of the card:
Greetings, our Vasya! We are all healthy, and wish you well. Here all is well, we are in our own house. All difficulties and dangers, thank God, will be over. We received a postcard from Vanko [Ivan Pidkalyuk—Wasyl's cousin]. We write to you every Sunday. Here it is already winter. My best wishes to you for the coming holidays of Christmas and the New Year . . .

Back of the card:
. . .that you be alive and healthy and that we shall soon see you and all live together. Vasya, we have lived through and are living through great danger, but don't worry, God knows all. We beg you to watch over your health, so that you do not catch cold, because it is winter now. Watch over yourself, because there is no one there to remind you. Dress warm, cover your neck, wear boots, make trousers and a jacket for yourself from a blanket. Only God knows what will be with us. We received help in the amount of 620 *karbovantsi*. This will be for you. Ksenia did not receive anything. Zoska [Ksenia's daughter] is serving in [the village] Zelentsi [working with the Germans as a translator]. The *sel'rada* does not really bother us. We have paid all taxes. All is well as of now. Questionable refugees have not come here so far. We received your photo cards. Be well, dear son, write, though the postal service is weak. We wish you blessings and health. Father, Mother. November 28, 43. Goodbye.[6]

 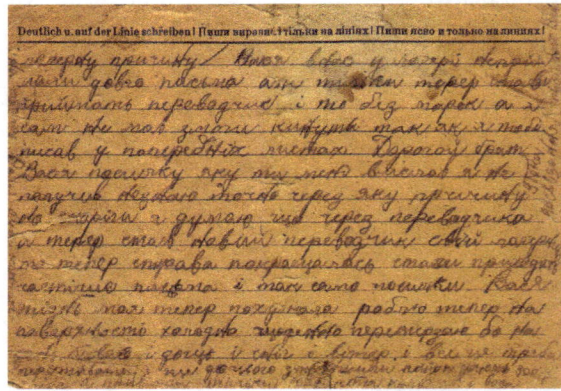

80. Postcard 23, dated February 16, 1944, front. 81. Postcard 23, dated February 16, 1944, back.

---

[6] This was a very difficult time. The Germans were retreating from Ukraine. People were afraid of what would happen.

Postcard 23. February 16, 1944

Front of the card:
To: Wasillii Kuschnir, Vert Marschalek, Mies—Isabental [sic], No. 474, Sudetengau [This was the address of Wasyl's new place of work at farmer Marschalek's.]
From: Ivan Pidkalyuk, No. 868, D.A.F. Lager Dalzburg, Zecke (Saar) (Saargruben)
Greetings, dear brother Vasya. In the first place, I want to tell you that I have received your latest letter as well as all others. Only, dear brother Vasya, I was sad because I could not respond to you, for two [unintelligible] written your letters and all [unintelligible]. . . .

Back of the card:
. . . situation with paper. Vasya, in our camp, they did not, for a long time, permit receipt of letters, and only now they began receiving a translator. We also have no postage stamps. And so I could not send you anything, as I have written to you in previous letters. Dear brother Vasya, I did not receive the package that you sent me. I don't know exactly why . . . [unintelligible], I think that it was because of the translator. But now there is a new translator, our own camp's translator, and the situation has improved, letters started arriving more often and packages as well. Vasya, my life has now grown thin. I am working now on the topside, every day it is cold, and I am freezing because . . . [unintelligible] there is rain, and snow, and wind, and I am just forced to suffer it all. We receive, for our work, thirty grams of bread and . . . [unintelligible] only watery soup, and [unintelligible], and water.

82. Postcard 24, dated May 7, 1944, front. 83. Postcard 24, dated May 7, 1944, back.

Postcard 24. May 7, 1944

Front of the card:
Vertical black and white image of three boys in uniforms marching with a swastika flag, a drum, and piccolo, with a girl waving to them, all at the base of a fortress tower. Over the scene there is a caption: "1935. DIE SAAR IST DEUTSCH FÜR IMMER" [THE SAAR IS FOREVER GERMAN].[7]

Back of the card:
Greetings, brother Vasya! In the first place, I want to tell you I currently find myself alive and well. I wish the same for you. Vasya, today is Sunday. It is a holiday, they allow us to play, and I also think of going out, so I'll throw you a little postcard. Vasya, I received your postcards, and I sincerely thank you for not forgetting about me. In a few days, I will write a letter to you and send you a photo of myself. Then I will describe my entire tragedy to you. With this, I end, until then, goodbye. Ivan.[8]

L to R: 84. Ivan Moiseievych Pidkalyuk with children Olha and Viktor. Unknown date and photographer. 85. Ivan Pidkalyuk's funeral, Chernyava, 1963. Unknown photographer.

---

7   The Saar is an area of Germany, occupied by the French and the British in the past.
8   Ivan Pidkalyuk, born in 1925, survived the war and died in 1963 in Ukraine.

The War Ends; I Am Set Free

By the end of the war, my farmer employer, Mr. Marschalek, received a directive from the police that I was to be freed immediately, and that I should go to the town of Mies, to the camp where they collected all of the forced laborers, wherever they came from, to return to their homeland. Mr. Marschalek paid me 200 Reichmarks and gave me my work book, to confirm that I worked for him. He also drove me to the camp, where I stayed for a week. Then, a train arrived, and we were loaded into the freight cars to travel east—to our homeland!

At the camp, I met several young men also from my village, Bubnivka. The train did not stop except at the border of Germany and Poland and in the Czechoslovakian city Dresden. Heading east, we stopped at the station. And here, heading west, stopped a train carrying soldiers from the Soviet Union. At the station, we told them who we were, and that we were going back to the motherland, and the Soviet soldiers started calling us names, "You fascists, you don't belong to any country, you will be sent straight to Siberia." And a big fight began.

From earlier years of Stalin's dictatorship and his NKVD and KGB, I knew that all returnees will be questioned as to who is who. I also had to consider the social situation in Nova Bubnivka, keeping in mind that the Kushnir family had been dispossessed and had been sent to Siberia and that my father had served with Petliura in the Ukrainian National Army. I knew that if the Soviets started questioning me, I would be sent straight to Siberia for ten years in a concentration camp.

I happened to meet a Ukrainian from Galicia, Dmytro Hrytsak, who had been in the "Galician Division" army. This so-called division was formed when the Germans had gathered Ukrainian young men to guard bridges and railroad tracks from Soviet partisans. These boys were marked with a tattoo under their arm, identifying their blood type, so they were easy to recognize. This young man was very afraid that he would fall into the hands of the KGB. When such boys were caught by the Soviets, they were immediately executed, or arrested and sent straight to the concentration camps in Siberia.

The Galician and I got to know each other and decided to leave our train to the homeland, by some means return to Germany, and get into the American zone. The Americans did not arrest anyone, and very few people were interrogated there. Moreover, free transportation was available in the American zone: all freight vehicles that stopped, military or civilian, would take on whoever wanted to travel from one town to another.

During the commotion caused by the fight between the soldiers and returning forced laborers from the two trains, Dmytro and I quietly walked off. We walked along the tracks until we met a German who worked on the railway. We told him that we wanted to return to the American zone. He advised us to hide in an empty car that the next day would be joined to a train of empty cars bound for the Czech city of Prague. From Prague it would be easier to travel to Bavaria, then in the American zone. And so we escaped from Dresden into Czechoslovakia. There, trains went on schedule, and we went from train to train, hiding as we had no tickets, until we "rabbits" got to the city of Regensburg in the American zone, which was at the time a big collection point for Ukrainian refugees.

Life in the Refugee Camp, Regensburg, Germany

The Regensburg refugee camp was located in the area called Ganghofer-Siedlung, previously named after Hermann Goering. Its inhabitants included Ukrainians like me who had worked as German forced laborers. Most of them did not want to be sent back to the Soviet Union, because, even though they had been taken by force by the Germans, a horrible fate would await them—execution or concentration camps in Siberia. However, shortly after I arrived, a Soviet officer had somehow persuaded the commander of the Regensburg camp to round up and deliver Ukrainians to the Soviet authorities. Military trucks surrounded the camp, some men were seized and taken into the trucks. Many Ukrainians, including myself, ran off into the surrounding forest and fields, hiding in ravines and anywhere else they could hide. A group of women, mostly wives of the men thrown into the trucks, lay down in front of the trucks, saying that if the authorities took their men, they would have to run over the women. The men were released, and no Ukrainian refugees from Regensburg were ever returned to the Moscow government. I understand that Mrs. Eleanor Roosevelt, wife of U.S. President Franklin Roosevelt, helped intercede on behalf of refugees who did not want to be returned to the USSR.

L to R: 86. Regensburg, Germany, circa 1947. Photograph by Wasyl Kushnir. 87. Ganghofer-Siedlung, circa 1947. Photograph by Wasyl Kushnir.

L to R: 88. Ukrainian Center, Regensburg, circa 1947. Photograph by Wasyl Kushnir. 89. Ukrainian Center, Regensburg, Circa 1947. Photograph by Wasyl Kushnir.

L to R: 90. Streets in Ganghofer-Siedlung, circa 1947. Photograph by Wasyl Kushnir. 91. Streets in Ganghofer-Siedlung, circa 1947. Photograph by Wasyl Kushnir.

After the war, various grassroots Ukrainian help organizations developed. One of them, the Ukrainian Committee, under the United Nations Relief and Rehabilitation Administration (UNRRA), provided support to refugees from Ukraine in Regensburg, including medical services, housing, food, places of worship, and all essential things needed for existence in post-war Germany. The Committee gave me a document that confirmed my desire not to return to Ukraine. It was an identification card with a photo, my name, family name, ID number, and my number as "Displaced Person." Once I had this document, there was no problem on the roads of Bavaria, with the German police and the American military police, the "Constabulary" of the Twelfth Corps, U.S. Army.

92. Identification document issued by Ukrainian Committee, August 24, 1945.

I also registered with the German police. I spoke German well by then, so I had no trouble with getting documents.

 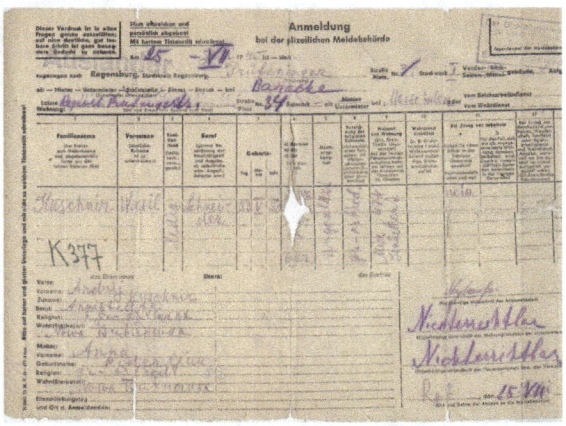

L to R: 93. Registration with German police, June 11, 1945. 94. Registration with German police, July 25, 1945.

    One time, when I got off from a car that had given me a ride, I realized that my leather wallet had been stolen by a pickpocket. It contained important papers—my Soviet passport and my German identification card—a small watch and some cash. I immediately went to the local police and was issued a temporary identification.

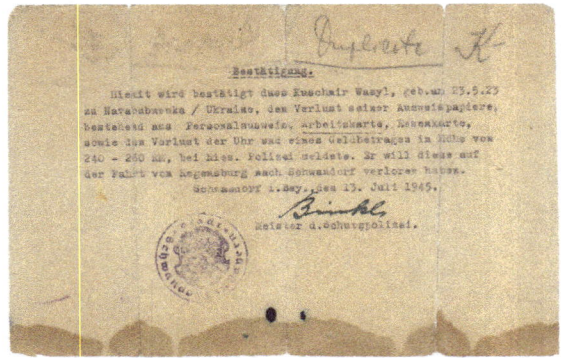

95. German police document confirming documentation was stolen, July 13, 1945.

Later, a more official temporary registration document was issued to me.

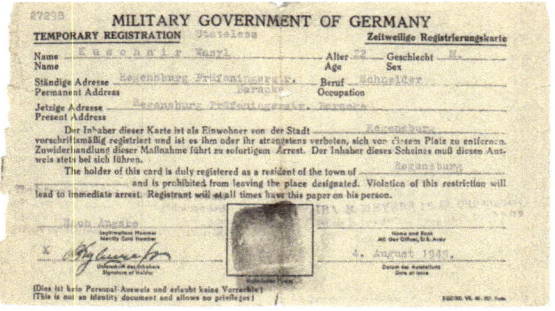

96. Temporary registration card, August 4, 1945.

By mid-August 1945, because I knew how automobile engines worked, I obtained a job driving trucks in Regensburg for Battery C 538 Field Artillery, Battalion, U.S. Army. There, I learned to drive various-sized trucks. Capt. Gauthier, the Commandant of Battery C, gave me good recommendations, and permitted me to enter and leave the military quadrangle, as well as to use the German Civilian Mess.

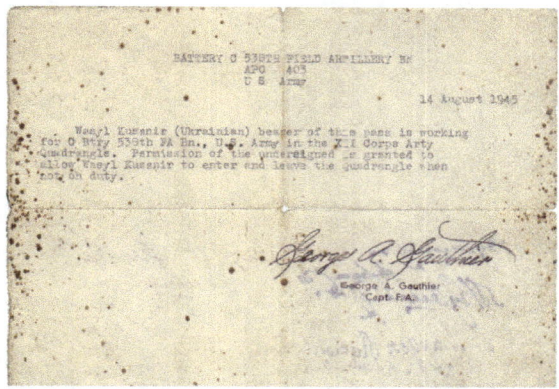

97. Permission to enter and leave the military quadrangle, signed Capt. George A. Gauthier, U.S. Army, August 14, 1945.

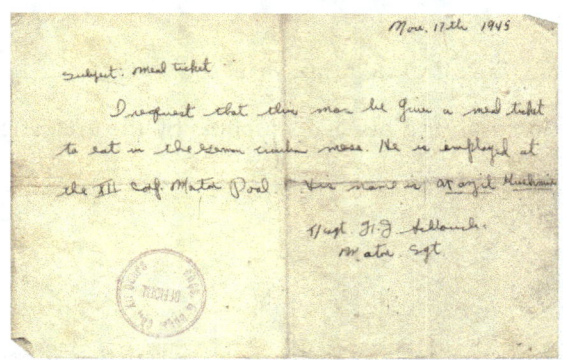

98. Permission letter, signed H. J. Schlouch, M. Sgt., U.S. Army, November 17, 1945.

The Americans were happy with my work. In a typed letter, Captain Gauthier stated:

Wasyl Kusznir (Ukrainian) has worked in Battery "C" 538th F.A. Bn. Motor Section for two months and proved extremely satisfactory in assisting in motor maintenance during that time. He is both energetic and honest and can be trusted without question. I recommend him highly to any unit in need of an assistant in their motor pool.

BDS Stationery, dated Oct. 2, 1945.

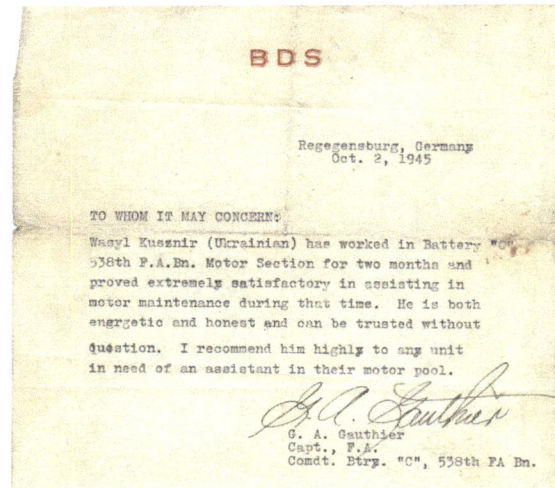

99. Recommendation letter, Capt. G. A. Gauthier, U.S. Army, October 2, 1945

I was also issued identification cards and other documents by the area engineer, and the Fourth Armored Division, U.S. Army.

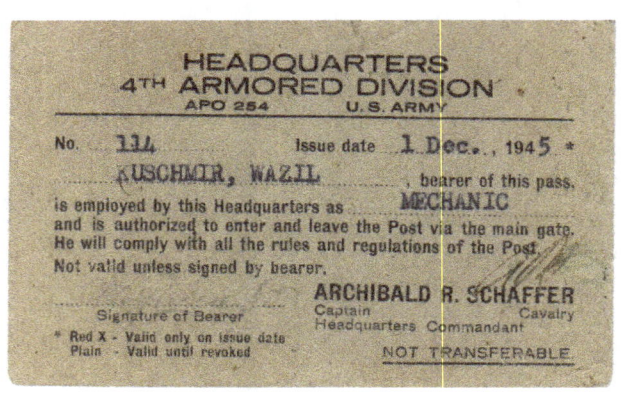 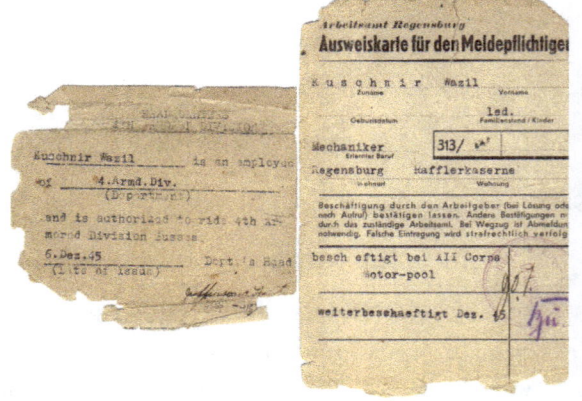

L to R: 100. Mechanic identification card, December 1, 1945. 101. Left, U.S. Army identification card fragment, dated December 6, 1945. Right, German identification card, undated.

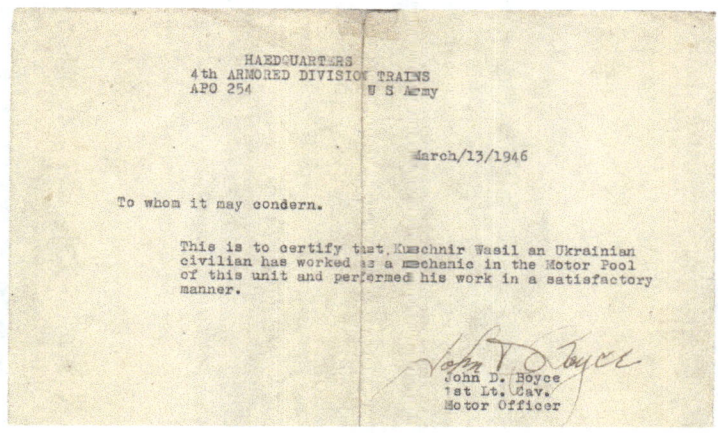

102. Recommendation, John D. Boyce, 1st Lt., Cav., U.S. Army, March 13, 1946

With the identification card received from the Ukrainian Committee in Regensburg, I qualified for German and American driver's licenses and vehicle operator permits to drive ¾- and 1½- to 2½-ton trucks.

L to R: 103. Wasyl Kushnir and other drivers, Headquarters, 1049 Labor Supervision Company, 1945. Unknown photographer.
104. Wasyl Kushnir with three other drivers, 1049 Labor Supervision Company, circa 1947–1948. Unknown photographer.

L to R: 105. Wasyl Kushnir, circa 1944. Unknown photographer. 106. Wasyl Kushnir with unknown man, circa 1945. Unknown photographer. 107. Wasyl Kushnir with an ambulance truck, 1945. Unknown photographer.

L to R: 108. Wasyl Kushnir, 1945. Unknown photographer. 109. Wasyl Kushnir, 1945. Unknown photographer. 110. Wasyl Kushnir, January 16, 1946. Unknown photographer.

L to R: 111. Wasyl Kushnir and 2¾-ton truck. Unknown date and photographer. 112. Wasyl Kushnir and 2¾-ton truck. Unknown date and photographer.

113. Wasyl Kushnir, Headquarters, 1049 Labor Supervision Company, Regensburg, 1948. Unknown photographer.

I also drove ambulance cars for UNRRA during this period. In addition, I worked for the 1049 Labor Supervision Company during 1947–48, and with Regensburg Military Office of the Motor Pool Officer, U.S. Army, until September 1949.

I Start My Own Family

In 1946, I met Maria Pawlishchiw, another Ukrainian farm worker taken by the Germans as a forced laborer. She had been conscripted along with her entire family. They came from Western Ukraine, selo Rudky, Rava-Ruska oblast. Her birth father had gone to France to work when she was a child, and the family soon lost contact with him. Her mother, Anastasia Pawlishchiw, later married to Petro Kosmyna, a widower, who had three children from his first wife: Mikhailo (oldest), Petrick (Petro), and Patricia. Petro wanted to keep the family together during the war, and so they had all been assigned to the same farm laborer work unit in Germany and were living in Regensburg after the war.

 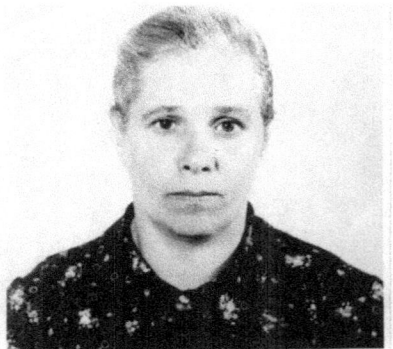

L to R: 114. Wasyl Kushnir and Petro Kosmyna, circa 1946. Unknown photographer. 115. Anastasia Pawlishchiw Kosmyna, circa 1945. Unknown photographer.

Maria was Ukrainian Greek Catholic, and a member of the Ukrainian Plast (Scout) organization. She was crossing the street one day, as I sat in my military truck, and she laughed back at me when I called for her to walk faster. After that, I started noticing her around the camp. She had a good sense of humor, was popular with her crowd and was quick with a response, whatever the situation.

L to R: 116. Plast girls in formation, Regensburg, circa 1945. Photograph by Wasyl Kushnir. 117. Maria (top) with friends, circa 1945. Photograph by Wasyl Kushnir.

L to R: 118. Maria Pawlishchiw, April 1942. Unknown photographer. 119. Maria in Plast uniform, July 22, 1946. Unknown photographer. 120. Maria, circa 1945. Photograph by Wasyl Kushnir.

Maria and I were married on August 1, 1946 in Regensburg. Our first son, Andrei, was born on August 30, 1947. I drove her, with my ambulance car, to the hospital and back to our apartment in the Regensburg camp. Andrei was christened in the camp, and his godfather, Petro Jarochym, gifted the baby carriage.

L to R: 121. Maria and Wasyl Kushnir, August 1, 1946, Regensburg, Unknown photographer. 122. Nurse and Maria Kushnir holding son Andrei, 1947. Photograph by Wasyl Kushnir.

L to R: 123. Maria and Andrei Kushnir, circa 1948. Photograph by Wasyl Kushnir. 124. Andrei Kushnir with rabbits, Regensburg, circa 1948. Photograph by Wasyl Kushnir.

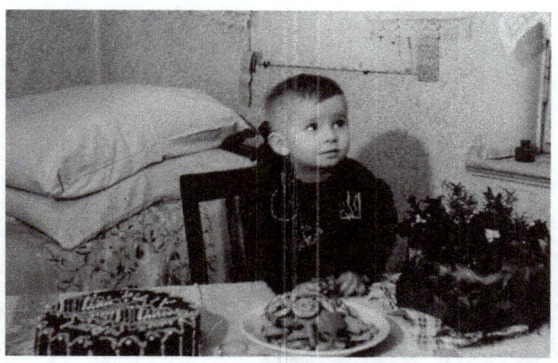 

L to R: 125. Andrei Kushnir, circa 1948. Photo by Wasyl Kushnir. 126. Maria, Andrei and Wasyl Kushnir, circa 1948. Unknown photographer.

I continued to work as a driver in the Regensburg Military Motor Pool, U.S. Army, until early September, 1949, when we moved to Amberg, in anticipation of emigrating from Germany. When I resigned, my supervisor, William, R. Gentry, provided me with a "Commendation of Services" letter, which confirmed my employment and my driver's qualifications. My work was characterized as "beyond reproach."

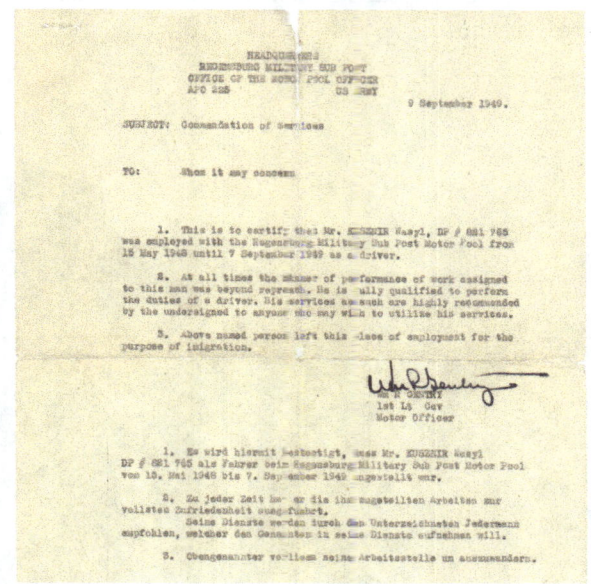

127. Commendation letter, by Wm. R. Gentry, 1st Lt. Cav. Motor Officer, U.S. Army, September 9, 1949.

Maria, Andrei, and I went to Amberg by train, together with her family.

128. Boarding the train to Amberg, Germany. First row left to right: unknown woman, unknown man, Petro Kosmyna (with hat), Anastasia Kosmyna, Maria Kushnir holding Andrei Kushnir, unknown woman, Petrick Kosmyna. Unknown boy and woman in front. Photograph by Wasyl Kushnir.

129. Train from Regensburg to Amberg, Germany, 1949. Photograph by Wasyl Kushnir.

I Start My Own Family

Our second son, Anatolij, was born in Amberg on November 19, 1949, while we were waiting to emigrate from Germany. We christened him in Amberg. Anatolij's godmother was Petro Jarochym's wife, Lusya (short nickname for Elisabeth).

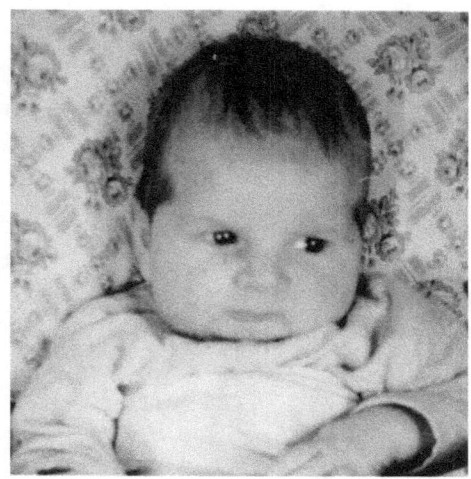 

L to R: 130. Anatolij Kushnir. Photograph by Wasyl Kushnir. 131. Wasyl and Maria Kushnir, with Andrei (carried) and Anatolij (in baby carriage), Amberg, 1949. Photograph by Petro Jarochym, Andrei's godfather.

We Immigrate to the United States

Many of our Ukrainian friends emigrated from Germany to locations all over the world, and we were eager to follow them. But first, we needed a sponsor. One day, we were told that a sponsor was found: a farm company called Delta & Pine Land Company in Scott, Mississippi, in the USA.

132. SAS airplane on which we flew to the United States, March 1, 1950. Photograph by Wasyl Kushnir

We flew to the United States on March 1, 1950 and arrived in New York, with stops in England and Newfoundland. The United Ukrainian American Relief Committee (ZUDAK) gave us $100 cash. With $72 of this money, we purchased bus tickets on March 8, 1950 to travel to our sponsor in Mississippi.

Our bus trip was memorable. Anatolij was still breastfed, and we had only two diapers, which we washed at rest stops. We sat at the bench seat in the back of the bus, so that we could all be together, to the stares of the other passengers on the bus. The further south the bus drove, the more destitute the inhabitants, mostly African Americans, appeared. It was a chill winter, but the cabins we drove by often had their front doors open, with a log sticking out. Evidently, the custom was to slowly push this log into the fireplace, burning it from one end.

When we arrived at our destination, I purchased living essentials in the company store, including a bed, bedsprings, mattress, stove, bucket, axe, shoes, and food. Thus, we were immediately $57.15 in debt.

133. Bus tickets to Mississippi, account, and receipt for purchases at Delta & Pine Land Co, 1950.

Scott, Mississippi was a very small village. Most of the population in the surrounding area were African Americans. The Delta & Pine Land Company gave us a small recently built wooden cabin to live, raised above the ground on stilts. Maria's parents lived with us. There was only one room, so space was tight, but we had few possessions, and we felt comfortable together. Our relatives—Maria's half-sister Patricia (Kosmyna) Karpa, her husband Wolodymyr Karpa, and their daughter Maria—lived nearby. My wife Maria planted watermelons, onions, and other vegetables. It was far to a store, so people had their own gardens.

Initially, the supervisor gave us jobs digging ditches, pulling weeds, and seeding cotton. Having worked for the Americans in Germany, I understood the English language fairly well. When I told the supervisor that I was a car mechanic and driver, he assigned me to work in the company's car and tractor maintenance shop, repairing starters and generators. If a tractor got stuck in the field, I was sent out to fix it or replace the parts. I earned 35 cents per hour, and Maria worked in the fields at 25 cents per hour. We earned $16 per week, kept $4 for ourselves, and the rest we gave back to the company to pay off our debt.

L to R: 134. Delta & Pine Land Company, Scott, Mississippi, photographer Marion Post Wolcott. Public Domain. 135. Delta & Pine Land Company, Scott, Mississippi, 1939. Courtesy of The New York Public Library, Schomburg Center for Research in Black Culture, Photographs and Prints Division.

136. Photograph of the Karpa family by Wasyl Kushnir, circa 1950.

I had heard about a Ukrainian community in Chicago and contacted them. They were very supportive and suggested I move to Chicago. When I told the supervisor at Delta & Pine Company that I was thinking of moving, he immediately offered me a house closer to where I worked and a car. But we were out of place in Mississippi and I decided that we should save enough money to move to Chicago.

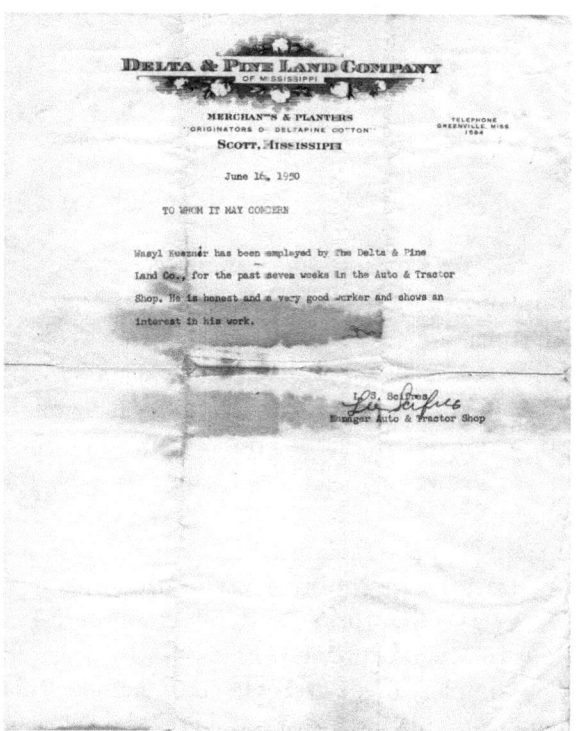

137. Letter of recommendation for Wasyl Kushnir issued by Delta & Pine Land Co., June 16, 1950.

Despite my wanting to leave so soon after arriving, Delta & Pine gave me a good letter of recommendation: "Wasyl Kusznir has been employed by the Delta & Pine Land Co., for the past seven weeks in the Auto & Tractor Shop. He is honest and a very good worker and shows an interest in his work. [Signed: L. S. Scifres, Manager, Auto & Tractor Shop]." Letter dated June 16, 1950.

Life in Chicago

On June 1, 1950, I left Mississippi by bus for Chicago, where other recently emigrated Ukrainians had moved with the support of St. Volodymyr Ukrainian Orthodox Cathedral, located at 2250 West Cortez St. The church meeting hall had been converted to a sleeping area for newly arrived immigrants. I slept on a cot there for about a week until I found work. Generally, the Ukrainians who already had a home and a job in Chicago came to the church to find laborers. One of people who came to look for laborers owned a pharmacy on nearby corner of Chicago Avenue and Oakley Boulevard. My first job, lasting two weeks, was post digging and constructing a fence for his brother in Indiana. While I was working there, one laborer killed a snake, and I remember that the owner of the property got angry because killing the snake upset nature.

At my request, Delta & Pine Land Company provided me with a recommendation. In the letter dated June 16, 1950, the manager of the car and tractor shop confirmed that I had been employed with them for seven weeks, saying about me: "He is honest and a very good worker, and shows an interest in his work." Soon, I found steady work in Chicago with Merit Hardware Manufacturing Company, which mostly hired immigrants. Their office was located on 2125 W. Rice St. The company made casket handles, nameplates and ornaments. I operated metal plating equipment, cleaned the metal, and dipped it into acid baths. The work area was very hot, full of noxious steam and gases. I would come home from work and immediately fall asleep, even during dinner. My skin turned a yellow color, and I lost so much weight that friends worried about me.

I earned $1.10 per hour at Merit Hardware. However, I saved enough and on January 12, 1951, I paid off all of our debts by check to the Delta & Pine Land Company.[1] I could even send money to Maria, for bus tickets to Chicago. Maria, our sons, and her parents, joined me in Chicago in June 1951. For about two months, we lived in spaces provided by the Chicago Ukrainian Committee on N. Western Avenue. Then, we moved to an apartment on 1511 N. Milwaukee Avenue, over a Goldblatt's Appliances store. We lived on the second floor, which had been divided into apartments with thin walls made from cardboard boxes.

---

1   The Delta & Pine Land Company is still in existence at the time of publishing this book, but the cotton fields had been sold off, and it operates as a research institution. Wasyl's son Andrei visited the locale in the Delta, in late 2018, for a video shot by photographer Gregory Staley about Andrei's paintings related to his family's experiences in Mississippi. Other than documents his father had preserved, they found little physical evidence of the family's living and work environment there. See https://www.youtube.com/watch?v=3VM9cmlH4iA.

L to R: 138. The building at 1511 N. Milwaukee Avenue, 2012. Photograph by Andrei Kushnir. 139. Milwaukee Avenue, from the 1511 building, looking north, also 2012. Photograph by Andrei Kushnir.

With the money I made from working at the metal plating factory, I purchased a used 1941 Chrysler automobile from Roxy Auto Sales, on W. Division St., for $561.00, including sales tax.

140. Anatolij, Andrei, and Maria Kushnir, with Chrysler, on Potomac St., 1952. Photograph by Wasyl Kushnir.

L to R: 141. Andrei, Maria, and Anatolij Kushnir, 1952. Photograph by Wasyl Kushnir. 142. Maria with Andrei and Anatolij Kushnir in Wicker Park, Chicago, 1953. Photograph by Wasyl Kushnir.

143. Anastasia and Petro Kosmyna. Photograph by Wasyl Kushnir.

Later that year, we moved to a house nearby at 1735 N. Potomac St., where we also lived on the second floor. My in-laws lived on the third floor, and Maria's brothers and her sister's family lived in the same building. The building's American owners also lived in an apartment on the third floor. When they purchased the first television set in our building, the owners invited everyone to come up to see it. The television sat with its screen facing up in a cabinet, and a mirror reflected the picture.

Our street was dead-ended at both sides. On the western side of the street there was a Polish union building that at one time had been a Jewish orphans home. On the eastern side there was a vacant lot over which went the elevated tracks of the Chicago "L" city transit system.

L to R: 144. Maria, Anatolij and Andrei Kushnir on stairs, 1735 Potomac Street. Photograph by Wasyl Kushnir. 145. Our block on Potomac Street, 1950s. Photograph by Wasyl Kushnir.

From 1951 to 1959, I worked at the Victor Gasket and Oil Seals Co., on the South Side of Chicago. I started as a janitor, then became a helper distributing parts to the presses that made complicated gaskets and oil seals. The work was hard and the workplace was hot, but the air was clean, as there were no acid fumes. I earned $1.50 per hour, or $2.00 per hour when I loaded the presses. Maria, worked at Electrical Fixtures Assembly Co., near our home on Potomac Street, assembling electrical components, part time, from September 1, 1952 to May 1, 1956. In 1953, we sold the Chrysler and purchased a new Ford automobile.

146. Maria, Anatolij, and Andrei Kushnir, with new Ford in Humboldt Park, 1953 or 1954. Photograph by Wasyl Kushnir.

In 1954, we bought the property two houses down the block at 1731 W. Potomac Street. It consisted of five apartments in two buildings, one behind the other. Our family lived on the second floor in the front, brick building. I installed gas heaters in the building and hot water tank and bath tub in our apartment. In March 1957 we purchased a three-flat brick building at 2734 W. Haddon Avenue in Chicago, where we moved into the apartment on the second floor. We sold the 1731 W. Potomac Street property in 1958.

147. 1731 W. Potomac Street, Chicago, Illinois. 2012. Photograph by Andrei Kushnir.

L to R: 148. 2734 Haddon Avenue, Chicago, Illinois. 1957. Photograph by Wasyl Kushnir. 149. Living room at 2734 Haddon Ave., circa 1958. Photograph by Wasyl Kushnir.

On September 1, 1957, our daughter Nadia was born.

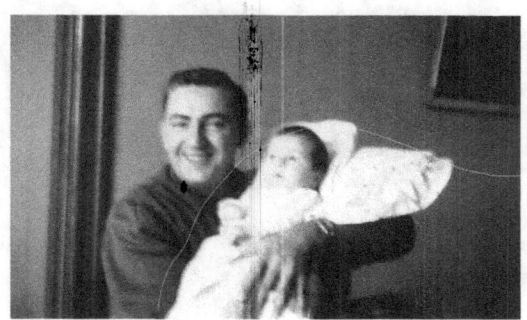 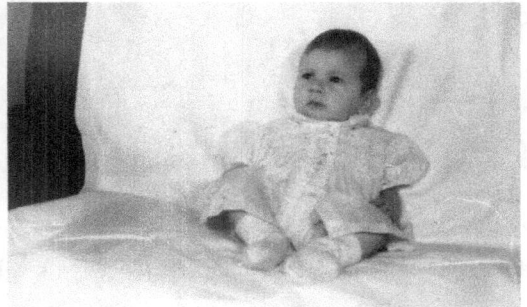

L to R: 150. Wasyl and daughter Nadia, 1957. Photograph by Maria Kushnir. 151. Nadia Kushnir, circa 1958. Photograph by Wasyl Kushnir.

152. Anatolij, Nadia, Maria, and Andrei, 1957. Photographer Wasyl Kushnir.

During all our time in Chicago, we were parishioners at St. Volodymyr Ukrainian Orthodox Cathedral, where I had first stayed after arriving from Mississippi. We attended church services every Sunday, and Nadia was christened there in 1957. Her godparents were Mykola Ilyashenko and Valentina Zapototskii. Mykola had also been Anatolij's godfather, and we knew both Mykola and Valentina from our days in Regensburg. Our children all went to the church's Sunday school and the Ukrainian school, which was held on Saturday mornings. In higher grades, they also had Ukrainian classes on weeknights.

L to R: 153. St. Volodymyr Ukrainian Orthodox Cathedral, corner of Oakley and Cortex Streets. Unknown date and photographer. 154. St. Volodymyr Parish Ukrainian School, 1965. Unknown photographer.

L to R: 155. Anatolij's First Communion, St. Volodymyr Parish, Pastor: Very Rev. Fedir Bilecky, 1956. Photograph by Wasyl Kushnir. Anatolij is in the white shirt, on left side. 156. Christening of our daughter Nadia at St. Volodymyr Ukrainian Orthodox Cathedral, Pastor: Very Rev. Fedir Bilecky. Photograph by Wasyl Kushnir.

L to R: 157. Ukrainian language student concert, Church Hall, St. Volodymyr Ukrainian Orthodox Cathedral, circa 1956. Photograph by Wasyl Kushnir. 158. Ukrainian language play, Church Hall, St. Volodymyr Ukrainian Orthodox Cathedral, circa 1966. Photograph by Wasyl Kushnir.

159. Ukrainian language poetry reading, Church Hall, St. Volodymyr Ukrainian Orthodox Cathedral, circa 1966. Photograph by Wasyl Kushnir.

160. Andrei's Ukrainian class at St. Volodymyr Ukrainian Orthodox Cathedral, circa 1966. Unknown photographer. Andrei is in the white shirt in the middle of the back row. The teacher, Prof. Antin Kushchynskij, is on the right at the end of the row.

My wife and I joined the St. Volodymyr Cathedral's Parents Committee, and I was elected its head in the late 1960s. Our children also participated in the cathedral's Ukrainian School plays, and concerts. They were also members of the Ukrainian Orthodox League. Our daughter took piano lessons, and our older sons (we later had a third son, Wolodymyr) joined the Ukrainian Democratic Youth Association (ODUM), where they sang in the bandurist choir or played in the string orchestra. Our family participated in demonstrations in support of a free Ukraine during Captive Nations Week in the United States, and other similar events. Anatolij and Nadia attended a Ukrainian Plast summer camp. Our family donated to the establishment of the united Ukrainian Orthodox Church in the USA. As part of this project, St. Andrew Memorial Church, Boundbrook, NJ, was erected, dedicated to the memory of 7–14 millions Ukrainians who perished in Stalin's Holodomor.

L to R: 161. Captive Nations parade, circa 1958. Photograph by Wasyl Kushnir. 162. Captive Nations parade, circa 1958. Photograph by Wasyl Kushnir.

L to R: 163. Captive Nations parade, circa 1958. Photograph by Wasyl Kushnir. 164. Captive Nations parade, circa 1958. Photograph by Wasyl Kushnir.

   Every year, we took a family vacation. In the early and mid-1950s, we visited Andrei and Anatolij's godparents, the Jarochyms and Ilyashenkos, who now lived in Maine and New Jersey. In the late 1950s and 1960s we vacationed in Wisconsin, staying with friends, the Czaikas, who owned a farm near Hayward, or at the Ballaugh's (now Red's) Big Bear Lodge in Winter, along the Flambeau River. We also vacationed in Minnesota, Florida, and Washington, D.C. Our whole family liked to fish, and pick raspberries, which were plentiful in Wisconsin in August, or apples and blueberries at nearby Indiana farms.

L to R: 165. Katerina Ilyashenko (Andrei's godmother), holding Andrei, Wasyl Kushnir, Maria Kushnir (holding Anatolij), July 8, 1951 in Newark, NJ. Photograph by Mykola Ilyashenko. 166. Kushnir Family, Fishing in Wisconsin, 1957. Photograph by Mykola Ilyashenko.

167. Anatolij, Andrei, and Maria Kushnir on a Wisconsin farm owned by family friends, the Czajka family, 1956. Photograph by Wasyl Kushnir.

I also enjoyed going to nearby Humboldt Park with Andrei and Anatolij to hit and catch baseballs. The boys wanted good baseball mitts, and we spent a whole day shopping for baseball gloves at Sears and Montgomery Wards department stores in Chicago. In winter we enjoyed ice skating and visiting museums.

L: 168. Anatolij and I went ice skating on the Humboldt Park lagoon in winter. Photograph by Andrei Kushnir. R: 169. When Andrei took up playing the guitar, we shopped in downtown Chicago until we bought just the guitar he wanted. Photograph by Anatolij Kushnir.

Reconnecting with my Mother

In the late 1950s, we were able to establish contact with my mother, Anna, in Ukraine, and learned, through her letters, that my father, Andrei, had died in March 1944. He had been arrested by the Communist authorities when the Germans retreated past their home in their village, Nova Bubnivka. He escaped from his cell, and, together with my mother, they were trying to reach the border from Nova Bubnivka on foot. They got as far as a village called Shatava and were walking in a column of refugees, when, according to my mother, a Bolshevik airplane sent to kill the refugees dropped a bomb, which blew my father's leg off. He bled to death and was buried in a mass grave with others killed by the airplane attack on unarmed, fleeing civilians. My mother became very ill, and a man from Shatava took her into his basement, where he spent a week nursing her back to health with only tea. Afterwards, she returned to Nova Bubnivka, where she lived with my paternal grandmother, Yaryna, until her death at age ninety-five in the mid-1950s. We corresponded with my mother until 1966, when, after much effort, I was able to assist her to immigrate to the United States.

170. Photograph of my grandmother Yaryna and Anna Kushnir, circa 1956. Unknown photographer.

Family Life in Chicago

Raising our family in Chicago, Maria, the children, and I did everything together. We erected kitchen cabinets, laid floors, and painted our apartments and the apartments we rented out. I could fix almost any mechanical thing, installed boilers and furnaces, automobile and motor boat engines, and I was not afraid of complicated plumbing and electrical jobs. When we painted a hallway or room, we would often joke, that "these are the 'good old days.'" They really were the good old days! While Maria and I kept a fairly strict household, where everyone knew their chores, I think the children felt free to be creative and enjoy their own lives. Our children have always been our most important focus in life, and we gave each of them all our love and attention.

171. Anatolij, Wasyl, Wolodymyr, Nadia, circa 1964. Photograph by Andrei Kushnir.

L to R: 172. Nadia, 1961. Photograph by Wasyl Kushnir. 173. Nadia's birthday party, 1965. Photograph by Wasyl Kushnir.

174. Nadia and Wolodymyr, circa 1962. Photograph by Wasyl Kushnir.

My wife Maria was an excellent cook. She prepared Ukrainian traditional dishes for Christmas Eve and Easter. For everyday meals, she cooked Ukrainian as well as American-style food, such as pork chops, pizza, fish, and steaks. In America, food was plentiful and cheap, so all our children were healthy and grew strong. Maria was also a great seamstress, and often sewed her own dresses, Nadia's clothing, drapes for the windows, and slipcovers. Maria also spent time with the children during the day when I had to be at work. In the evenings, the children studied. On weekends, our family went to church, church sponsored events and concerts. Maria and her mother would often get together to make traditional Ukrainian *varenyki* [boiled cheese, cabbage or potato dumplings] or *holubtsi* [cabbage rolls]. When my mother, Anna, emigrated from Ukraine in 1966, she would join them on Saturdays.

After our house on 1731 Potomac Street sold in 1958, the Polish real estate broker who handled the transaction, Thaddeus W. Krawczyk, told me that since I spoke fluent Polish, I could be a good salesman for his Polish clients. And so, after studying, I obtained a Real Estate Salesman license.

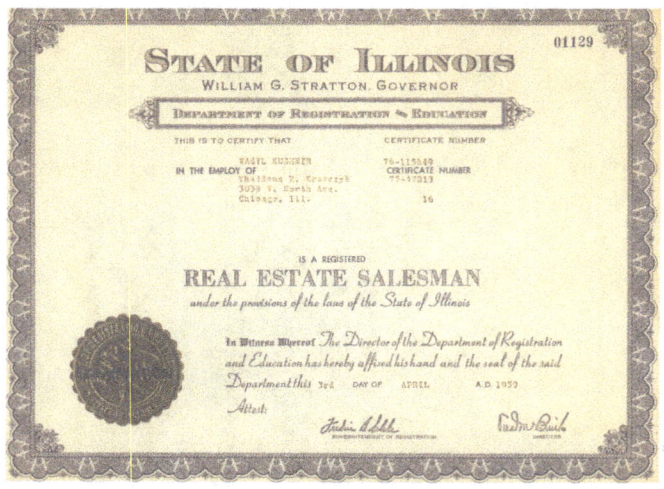

175. Wasyl Kushnir, Real Estate Salesman license, April 3, 1959.

In 1959, I went to work as a real estate salesman at Krawczyk's Humboldt Realty on West North Avenue and North Sacramento Street, across the street from Humboldt Park. I had a desk and a phone in his office. Krawczyk and his team of salesmen read the advertisements about houses on sale, and called the people, telling them that the company serviced the Polish community and had ready buyers. My job was to list houses and show them to clients. I always dressed well and was on time. Krawczyk encouraged the salesmen to work hard, and gave us helpful advice. I recall that some men came to our office once and demanded protection money from Krawczyk, but he loudly asked them to leave the office and threatened to call the police. I later found another job in real state with Park Realty, also on West North Avenue, a block away. The broker there was Alexander (Alex) Nimczenko, a Ukrainian friend from our church. He was very professional and knowledgeable in the real estate business. In both offices, I sold many properties to immigrants of many nationalities, such as Ukrainian, Polish, Puerto Rican, Jewish, Armenian, or Russian, as well as to American-born clients. At Park Realty, we managed some buildings in rougher parts of Chicago, and I sometimes accompanied Alex to collect rents.

Much of the real estate business took place on weekends, so, to my disappointment, I did not have as much time as before for our family. However, Maria ensured that the children continued attending Ukrainian school, do their homework, and treated them to shows at the neighborhood movie theaters on Sunday afternoons.

On June 13, 1961, our son Wolodymyr was born. Alex Nimczenko became his godfather.

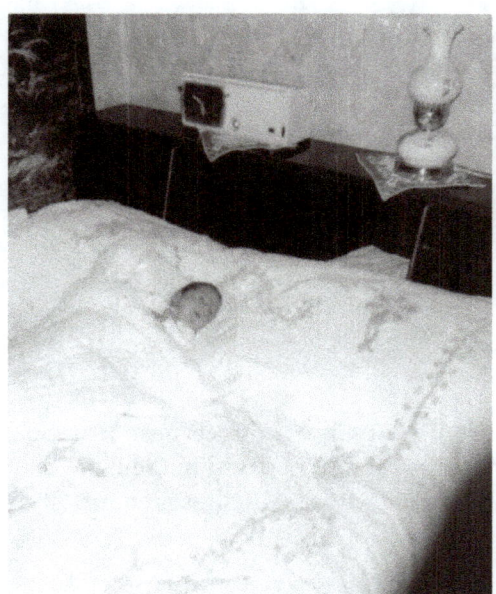 

L to R: 176. Wolodymyr, June, 1961. Photograph by Wasyl Kushnir. 177. Wolodymyr, 1970. Photograph by Wasyl Kushnir.

In 1963, we sold the house on Haddon Avenue, and moved to a rented apartment on 3317 West Hirsch Street, a little over a mile away, on the other side of Humboldt Park. After a few months, we purchased a house at 2525 North St. Louis Avenue. This was a two-story brick building, with three flats and a full basement. We lived in the first-floor apartment and rented the two apartments upstairs.

178. The building at 2525 N. St. Louis Ave. Photograph by Wasyl Kushnir

In 1964 we purchased a brick and frame building at 3339 West Crystal Street, near Humboldt Park. The building contained two apartments, which we rented out. When my mother arrived in the United States in 1966, she lived with us, and for a period with my mother in-law, Anastasia, who lost her husband in 1970, in one of the apartments at the property on Crystal Street, until Anastasia passed away in 1972.

179. The building at 3339 West Crystal Street. Photograph by Wasyl Kushnir

180. Anastasia Kosmyna, Nadia Kushnir, Anna Kushnir, circa 1968. Photograph by Wasyl Kushnir.

181. The Kushnir Family, circa 1968. Front row: Wolodymyr, Anna, Nadia. Back row: Andrei, Maria, Wasyl and Anatolij. Photographer: Darc Studios, Chicago, no successor in interest.

In 1964, my sons Andrei, Anatolij, and I attended the unveiling of the Taras Shevchenko monument in Washington, D.C. There, we saw President Dwight D. Eisenhower, who had approved the monument, speak at the ceremony. We also attended the associated banquet, where one of the main speakers was Ukrainian-American actor Jack Palance.

All our children attended public schools from kindergarten through college, except Nadia, who went to a private high school. All four children finished university and received Bachelor degrees. Andrei also earned a Master Degree in Government and a Law Degree, Anatolij attained a Law Degree, Nadia earned a Master Degree in Business Administration, and Wolodymyr, our youngest, earned his Bachelor Degree in Electrical and Civil Engineering.

In 1968, we purchased a three-story brick building with eight apartments at 2143–45 West Chicago Avenue. We rented out all the apartments and took on the responsibility for maintaining them. I installed electrical doorbells for all the apartments in this building.

182. The building on Chicago Avenue, circa 2014. Photographer unknown.

Later in 1968, after attending night school, I received a certification for High School equivalency from Wells High School, and obtained a Real Estate Broker license from the State of Illinois. I created my own real estate company, Union Realty, and became an independent broker.

183. Wasyl Kushnir, Real Estate Broker License, May 9, 1968.

In 1971, Maria and I celebrated our twenty-fifth wedding anniversary. Close friends surprised us with a party.

184. Twenty-fifth wedding anniversary party, 1971. Photograph by Bohdan Chomko.

Move to Palatine, Illinois

In 1975, my wife Maria and I purchased a building and 1.75 acres of land at 1016 South Smith Street, Palatine, Illinois. We lived there with my mother Anna, daughter Nadia, and son Wolodymyr. We planted fruit trees and grape vines, many varieties of berries, and a vegetable garden. We also created an apiary, and the bees produced enough honey for our own use.

185. Wasyl Kushnir in orchard at Palatine, Illinois property, circa 1980. Photograph by Wolodymyr Kushnir.

L to R: 186. Anna Kushnir, circa 1980. Photograph by Wasyl Kushnir. 187. Andrei's in-laws, Stefan and Anna Shyshko, with Wasyl Kushnir, on the Palatine, Illinois property, circa 1980. Photograph by Andrei Kushnir.

In 1984, I became a Notary Public in Cook County, Illinois.

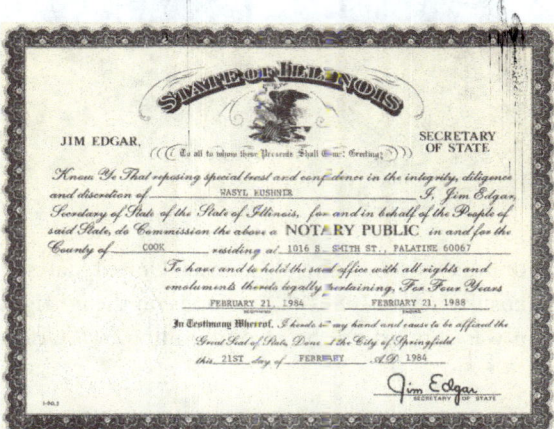

188. Wasyl Kushnir, Notary Public Certificate, February 21, 1984

After our move to Palatine, Illinois, we became members of the St. Andrew Ukrainian Orthodox Church in Bloomington, Illinois. My mother is buried in that church's cemetery. She died in 1988, at the age of eighty-six.

Our Family in America

Our sons, Andrei and Anatolij, both worked for the United States Government as attorneys.

L to R: 189. Andrei was an attorney with the Office of General Counsel, United States Navy, and one of his assignments was Counsel, U.S. Naval Supply Depot, Yokosuka, Japan 1984–86. Andrei is on the far right, first row. Unknown photographer. 190. One of Andrei's projects in Japan was supporting the reconditioning of a United States Navy aircraft carrier, 1986. Unknown photographer.

Andrei also undertook a career as an artist. He has painted landscapes all over the United States and other parts of the world.

191. Andrei Kushnir painting in Telluride, Colorado, 2017. Photograph by Tash Montlake. Permission granted.

Anatolij was elected as a member of the U.S. Senior Executive Service (the senior level of U.S. Government service under Presidential appointees). In the 2010s he was Associate Administrator for Acquisitions and Installations at the U.S. Department of Veteran Affairs.

L to R: 192. Anatolij Kushnir, Attorney, U.S. Department of Interior, 1973. Unknown photographer. 193. Anatolij Kushnir, 2010. Unknown photographer.

Our family never forgot its heritage. Andrei's children Larissa and Basil attended a Ukrainian-language school in Washington, D.C., and participated in memorial celebrations honoring Ukraine's national poet, Taras Shevchenko.

L to R: 194. At the Taras Shevchenko monument, Washington, D.C., circa 1990. Unknown photographer. 195. Larissa acting in Ukrainian school play, circa 1991. Unknown photographer.

When Ukraine became an independent nation in 1991, Anatolij and Andrei organized an effort to renovate Ukrainian airports, supported by a consortium of large companies such as Raytheon, Celadon, British Airport Authority and Leo Daly Architects. Their consortium group organized a symposium about airport redevelopment, and met with the then-president of Ukraine, Leonid Kuchma, as well as senior members of Ukrainian military and other government representatives.

196. Anatolij (third from left in back row) and Andrei (fourth from left in front row) with the Rector of the National University of Internal Affairs, Colonel-General of Police, and National Deputy of Ukraine, Oleksandr M. Bandurka, 1993. Other members of the North American consortium were Michael Simmons, attorney (second from left in back row), Edward J. Melanson, former U.S. Ambassador (third from left in front row), and Gregory Shyshko, Canadian oil company executive (first from left in front row). Unknown photographer.

Our Move to Florida. The Family Grows

Because of the difficult winters in Illinois, Maria and I decided to move to Florida. In 1987 or 88, we purchased a lot and a mobile home at 8017 Fiat Avenue in Brooksville, Florida. We visited this place on vacation and lived there temporarily. In 1990, we sold the apartment building at 2143–45 West Chicago Avenue, and in 1992, we sold the building on Crystal Street. In 1993, we sold the property at 1016 South Smith Street, Palatine, Illinois, and moved to Florida, where, that year, we purchased a house at 100 Wilhelm Drive, Englewood Beach, Manasota Key, on the Gulf coast. Later, we purchased an adjoining lot behind our house. There, Maria has a nice garden, and we also have trees with tropical fruits, such as papayas, figs, mangos, oranges, and avocados. We love to go fishing in the Gulf of Mexico near our house, and our children visit us with their families. In 1996, they all surprised us, coming down to Florida to celebrate our fiftieth wedding anniversary. They organized a prayer service at the local Ukrainian church in Northport, Florida, and held a dinner at a nice restaurant in Englewood.

L to R: 197. Maria Kushnir, Englewood Beach, Forida, 2010. Photograph by Raissa Kushnir. 198. Wasyl Kushnir, Englewood Beach, Florida, 2010. Photograph by Raissa Kushnir

L to R: 199. Maria, Wasyl and Andrei Kushnir, Manasota Key, 2010. Photograph by Raissa Kushnir. 200. Maria and Wasyl Kushnir with daughter Nadia, Englewood Beach, 2013. Photograph by Raissa Kushnir.

Our children have all married spouses of Ukrainian descent, and we now have our own family in the United States.

L to R: 201. Andrei and wife Raissa, 1971. Unknown photographer. 202. Anatolij and wife Jaroslava, 1978. Photograph by Andrei Kushnir.

L to R: 203. Nadia and husband Bohdan, 1979. Unknown photographer. 204. Wolodymyr and wife Larysa, 2007. Photograph by Andrei Kushnir.

L to R: 205. Members of the Kushnir family in Englewood, Florida, August 1993. Back row, L to R: Bohdan Chomko (Nadia's husband), Wasyl, Anatolij, Jaroslava (Anatolij's wife). Middle row, L to R: Nadia holding son Gregory, Maria, Raissa (Andrei's wife). Front row, L to R: Larissa (Andrei's daughter), Basil (Andrei's son), Andrei, Wolodymyr. Photograph by Andrei Kushnir. 206. Members of the Kushnir family on the veranda in Englewood, Florida, 2012. Back row, L to R: Andrei, Wasyl, Anatolij, and Wolodymyr. Front row, L to R: Nadia, Raissa (Andrei's wife), Maria, Larysa (Wolodymyr's wife). Photograph by Andrei Kushnir.

L to R: 207. Grandson Basil, great granddaughter Sophie, Wasyl, Maria, great granddaughter Lilia, grandson Basil's wife Melissa, 2011. Photograph by Basil Kushnir. 208. Front row, L to R: Maria, daughter Nadia, grandson Gregory, Nadia's husband, Bohdan. Back row, L to R: Wasyl, Nadia's son Alexander, sons Andrei, Anatolij, Wolodymyr, Wolodymyr's wife Larysa, 2010. Photograph by Andrei Kushnir.

L to R: 209. The new generation: Gregory and Alexander, sons of our daugher Nadia and son-in-law Bohdan Chomko. Photograph by Anatolij Kushnir. 210. The new generation: Sophie, Anastasia, and Lilia, daughters of our grandson Basil and his wife Melissa. Photograph by Melissa Kushnir.

211. The new generation: Russell Andrei, son of our granddaughter Larissa and her husband Wesley Davis, 2015. Unknown photographer.

Return to Ukraine

In 1994, Maria and I visited our homeland, Ukraine, and spent three weeks there. We visited my cousin, Raissa Yaremchuk (who had written to me while I was a forced laborer in Germany) in Vinnytsya, Halyna and Vasyl Besarab in Try Krynytsi (with whom my mother and father had tried to relocate in the 1930s) near Odessa, and my cousin Viktor Pidkalyuk who also lived there. We travelled to the place of my childhood home in Nova Bubnivka and found that the house my father, Andrei, had built had been destroyed, and the site was covered with weeds. My grandmother Yaryna's house still stood, but it had been rebuilt. As I mentioned in the beginning of these recollections, we visited my grandfather Semen's grave in the Nova Bubnivka cemetery. Maria and I also spent time in Kyiv with my relatives, the Kosar family, and with Ms. Olha Vronska, principal of an elementary school in Kyiv. Ms. Vronska had previously travelled to the United States and participated in a teacher exchange program with our daughter-in law, Raissa. One of the highlights of our trip to Ukraine was taking a boat trip on the Dnipro River on the *strila* ["arrow"] from Kyiv to Kaniv to visit Taras Shevchenko's museum and gravesite.

L to R: 212. Taras Shevchenko's museum, Kaniv, 1994. Unknown photographer. 213. Olha Vronska and Maria Kushnir, 1994. Photograph by Wasyl Kushnir.

L to R: 214. Wasyl Kushnir, Golden Gate of Kyiv, 1994. Photograph by Maria Kushnir 215. Maria and Wasyl Kushnir, with two others, at Taras Shevchenko's gravesite monument, Kaniv, 1994. Unknown photographer.

Last Thoughts

I appreciate the kindness of the American people who provided a place for us to live in peace and freedom, with dignity and with many opportunities. This country welcomed the people of Ukrainian ancestry who could not live any longer in their homeland. By publishing this account, I hope to facilitate the understanding of the situation in Ukraine under Communist times. That system was built on, and institutionalized, lies and twisted history from beginning to end, with no hope for its citizens to even have an honest conversation with each other. In the free American society, a person's life is unbounded. Everyone who wants it can seek education and betterment in every sphere of life—economic, physical, and spiritual.

My life has never been easy, either in Ukraine, in Germany or here, in America. But the world is big, and with a little faith, luck, and health, I have learned that if things don't seem to go your way, you can try to avoid the bad. In this country, that seems absolutely possible, from my perspective. If you keep moving forward, day by day, there is a good chance that you can survive and create a good life for yourself and your family.

216. Maria and Wasyl Kushnir, Englewood, Florida, 2014. Photograph by Raissa Kushnir.

Postscript

In March 2017, Wasyl Kushnir's beloved wife, and our dear mother, Maria, suffered a massive stroke. Our father, my brothers, sister, and I sat at our mother's bedside for a heart wrenching week before she passed away. In September of the same year, a powerful hurricane, Irma, threatened the Florida Gulf Coast. My brothers Anatolij and Wolodymyr boarded up the Englewood house and, with our nephew Gregory Chomko, took our father inland near Wolodymyr's home in St. Petersburg, Florida, to weather out the storm. Our father's home suffered minimal damage, but the hurricane was the cause of much anxiety to all concerned. Thus, even so late in life, our father faced deep loss and great uncertainty. However, with the help of family, he rebounded from these events, though much debilitated by age and the batterings of life. On February 2, 2019, our father, Wasyl Kushnir, passed away in his sleep, three months before his 96th birthday.

    Our father remains an inspiration to his family, and a perfect example of the human ability to survive in the face of unbelievable hardships, through periods of danger, terror, sorrow, and uncertainty, across continents and epochs. His life story is an example of determination and persistence.

Andrei Kushnir

www.ingramcontent.com/pod-product-compliance
Lightning Source LLC
Chambersburg PA
CBHW082142230426
43672CB00016B/2935